The Puritans on the Lord's Supper

by

Richard Vines
Edmund Calamy
William Wadsworth
Joseph Alleine
Thomas Watson

Edited by Don Kistler

Soli Deo Gloria Publications
. . . for instruction in righteousness . . .

Soli Deo Gloria Publications
P.O. Box 451, Morgan, PA 15064
(412) 221-1901/FAX 221-1902

*

*

ISBN 1-57358-041-4

Contents

The Passover

*Its Significance, and the Analogy Between
it and Christ our Passover*

by Richard Vines

"For Christ our passover is sacrificed for us. Therefore let us keep the feast, not with old leaven."
1 Corinthians 5:7–8

The Lord's Supper began at the Passover, at the
death whereof, and out of the ashes of it. This
sacrament of ours, like another phoenix, arose, for
our Lord, at His last Passover, called it His dying
Passover. He instituted and ordained this sacrament,
which is to live and remain till He comes again,
and, as Scaliger and others have observed, the very
materials of our sacramental supper were taken out
of the Paschal supper; for that very bread which the
master of the family used by custom (not by any
Scripture command) to bless and give to the family,
saying, "This is the bread of affliction which the fathers did eat in Egypt," and that cup which he
blessed and gave them to drink, called "the cup of
the hymn," because the hymn followed after and
closed all—that bread and that cup Christ, according to the rite, blessed and gave, saying, "This is My
body; this cup is the new testament in My blood."
And so He put a new superscription or signification
upon the old metal, and let all blind and bold ex-

positors know that if they do not expound many phrases and things in the New Testament out of the old records of Jewish writings or customs, they shall give but their fancy, and not expound the text.

In handling the sacrament of the Lord's Supper, I begin with the Passover, which was the second (circumcision being the first) ordinary, standing sacrament of the Jewish church, beginning at their going forth out of Egypt and continuing till the death of Christ, when the Lord's Supper commenced or began, and so displaced it. The Passover signified what should be the Lord's Supper, what is fulfilled in Christ.

In the Passover, the sufferings and death of Christ were represented by a lamb slain and roasted with fire. In the Supper, they are represented by bread broken and wine poured forth. The outward symbols or signs differ, but Christ is the same under both. As circumcision was theirs and baptism ours, there are different signs and rites, but the inward circumcision and regeneration are both one. Theirs were both bloody sacraments, for the blood of Christ was to be shed; ours is unbloody, for the blood has been shed.

Our English well translates the word "passover," while the Greek and Latin keep the word "pascha," which gave some occasion to derive it from the Greek word which means "to suffer a mistake." The word is *pesach*, from *pasach*, which is "to leap or pass over." For when Israel, after long servitude in Egypt, was on the verge of being gone, God commanded them in the various families to kill a lamb or kid, to roast it whole, to eat it within doors that night, and to sprinkle the side and upper door posts with the blood, not the threshold, for Christ's blood must not be trampled on. In so doing they should be safe from the destroying angel who rode circuit that night to kill all Egypt's firstborn. But he passed over all the houses of Israel which were sprinkled with blood, and hence the name "Passover," the origin whereof is given by God Himself in Exodus 12:27. We have the kernel in this shell, the marrow of this bone. We have a passover as well as they, but ours is Christ. "Our Passover is Christ," says the text.

Our Passover, Christ, is or was sacrificed for us. Our Passover, Christ, was a true sacrifice, but whether their Passover was a sacrifice or not is in question. The papists swallow it greedily, hoping thereby to prove our Supper to be both a sacrifice and a sacrament as their Passover (they say) was. But there are others, both Lutherans and Calvinists, who do not consider the Passover a proper sacrifice, even though it is so called in Exodus 12:27: "It is the sacrifice of the Lord's Passover," for so both the Greek and Hebrew words are sometimes generally taken for *mactare* when there is no sacrifice. And they find in Egypt at the first Passover no priest, but the head of the family; no altar, no offering of the lamb to God, no expiation; nor is it necessary that it should *be* a sacrifice to be the *type* of a sacrifice, for the serpent on the pole signified Christ crucified, and so the Passover as a sacrament may represent a sacrifice, as our supper is the commemoration of a sacrifice, but not actually be a sacrifice.

On the other hand, Calvin and some Jewish writers hold it to be a sacrifice and a sacrament, for the

Scripture calls it "sacrifice," and this blood is shed at first by the head of the family, who was a priest (no other being yet consecrated), and in later times by the priests or Levites. The blood was brought to the altar, as it was blood shed for a religious end, a blood preservative from destroying angels, and therefore a proper sacrifice.

What shall we say? I promise not to puzzle you with controversies and disputes, for I would rather set meat before you which you may eat than hard bones to gnaw upon. The truth is, a sacrifice is something offered to God by men; a sacrament is offered and given to man by God to be eaten or used in His name. And so that part of the offering which is offered up to God may be called a sacrifice, and that part eaten or used by man is called a sacrament. The very body and blood of Christ was a sacrifice, not a sacrament. The bread and wine, as used, are a sacrament, not a sacrifice.

The Passover was the figure of a true sacrifice, Christ, and we may call it so because the Scripture does. It follows after "let us keep the feast." What is that? You shall find that after the Passover lamb was eaten, the next day began the feast (Numbers 28:16–17); and the Passover is called a feast too in Exodus 12:14, and that continued seven days, kept in great festivity and solemnity, but with unleavened bread. The Apostle alludes hereunto: "Our Passover is sacrificed; therefore let us henceforth . . . ." We who have received the sprinkling of blood, and eaten His flesh by faith, live all our days in a holy rejoicing and thanksgiving, which is a continual feast. And let us cast the incestuous Corinthian out of our society, for he is a leaven. 1 Corinthians 5:7: "And let us purge out of ourselves" (malice, wickedness, etc.), for they are leaven (verse 8), that we may be a holy congregation and a holy people. And so the argument of the Apostle stands from the example of the old Passover. Those for whom Christ, the Passover, is sacrificed ought, as holy congregations and holy people, to be unleavened with sin and wickedness, and to walk before God in an unleavened sincerity; but for us, Christ the Passover is sacrificed; therefore "let us keep the feast."

I have explained the words, and now we shall consider this Passover in two ways:

1. As a sacrifice or figure of a sacrifice, and so it refers to Christ our Passover. "Christ is sacrificed for us."

2. As a sacrament, and so it relates to us and shows us our duty upon that sacrifice. "Let us keep the feast." The sacrifice is given *for* us; the sacrament is given *to* us.

1. Our Passover is Christ sacrificed for us. We have a Passover, but it is Christ sacrificed. And here, before I show the analogy or resemblance between the Passover and Christ, we shall note three or four things:

(1) They in the old church of Israel had Christ as well (though not as clearly) as we. In 1 Corinthians 10:4, the Rock that followed our fathers in the wilderness was Christ; the Passover was Christ; the personal types (such as Isaac on the wood) and the real types (the bloody sacrifices) were Christ. He was then in His swaddling clothes, swathed up in

shadows and types, not naked. In the New Testament, those types, being anatomized and unbowelled, are full of gospel, full of Christ. Christ is the marrow in the bone, the kernel in the shell, "the same yesterday, and today, and forever," the sum and sweetness of all ordinances. Therefore, those who say these types were filled with temporal promises, but had no spiritual promises, derogate too much from them, as if they were swine filled with husks. It is a wondrous paradox that those who had so much faith (Hebrews 11) should have no Christ. We give them the right hand of fellowship, and they were the elder brother, but we have the double portion.

(2) Mark the form of speech: "Christ our Passover," that is, our Paschal Lamb, which is also called the Passover in Exodus 12:21: "Kill the Passover." Now the Passover properly was the angel's passing over the Israelites' houses, and not the lamb; but we must learn to understand sacramental phrases: the sign called is the thing signified, the figure called is the thing figured. The Rock was Christ, Christ our Passover, that is, our Paschal Lamb. Circumcision is called the covenant in Genesis 17:13: "My covenant shall be in your flesh." This understanding will be allowed in every place but one, and that is this one: "This is My body." For in this instance the Lutheran argues for a corporal presence under the signs, and the papist argues for a change of the bread and wine into Christ's body and blood. No conferences, no disputes, no condescensions will satisfy them; and yet we say very fairly that the very body of Christ, born of the virgin, who dies on the cross, who sits in heaven, is present in

this sacrament—but not in the bread or wine, but to the faithful receiver; not in the elements, but to the communicants.

But all this will not resolve the division. These two prepositions, *con* and *trans* (when put before "substantiation), have bred more strife and cost more blood since they were born (and neither is six hundred years old) than can be easily imagined.

(3) The Passover prefigured Christ, and yet the Jews ordinarily did not see Christ in it. It is plain that, in their celebration of the Passover, or their rituals, they take notice of and commemorate their Egyptian slavery and their deliverance, and so they were commanded; but of Christ there is not a syllable. It entered not into them that a lamb roasted should prefigure the Messiah, as they had formed Him in their thoughts, and so they held the Passover not looking backwards, but as a type looking forward, with no knowledge except for the faithful who had some glimpse of it. And this is the great fault of men in all sacraments: they mind not the inward meaning of a sacrament, nor look for the kernel. They failed to do so, and we do as well. Is it not rightly discerning the Lord's body that which makes us guilty of His body and blood? Earthly men see the earthly part. They eat, they drink, but it feeds them not. They eat shells, but the inward things within the bones are marrow, Christ. Christ sets spiritual food before our bodies. He sets corporal food before our souls.

(4) The Passover is Christ sacrificed, not Christ an unspotted Lamb, but Christ a Lamb roasted with fire. And this tells you that the Passover

and our Supper represent Christ crucified, Christ dying or dead. It is the death of Christ, not His resurrection or ascension, that is here set forth. "Ye show the Lord's death till He comes." This is the sight which a sinful soul would see; this is the comfortable spectacle, to see the price paid, the ransom laid down, the thing being done. Hence the soul draws the hope and comfort of redemption; and therefore the bread was broken and the cup was full of blood to represent to the life this life-giving death of Christ. The papists have cheated the people of the blood by a trick of concomitancy, telling them that the bread is His body and His body has blood in it. We have a word of institution of both severally: the life of the representation is the blood shed; the Passover is a lamb slain and roasted, and the blood on the doorpost. And by providence, if the papists will allow all to eat, then we have expressly for the cup Matthew 26:27: "Drink ye all of it."

So that it is the death of Christ here represented, and, which is one step further, it is a sacrificial death, which works and makes atonement. This was what all the sacrifices that the Passover prefigured: a sacrificial death that would deliver and make expiation. "This cup," said Christ, "is the new testament in My blood, which is shed for you and many for remission of sins." It is a death, and such a kind of death as in our sacrament is set forth as a sacrificial death; therefore it is said that Christ is "sacrificed for us."

The Resemblance between the Passover and Christ Sacrificed

Now let us come to the analogy or resemblance between the Passover and Christ sacrificed, wherein I shall endeavor to avoid the vanity and curiosity of making too many similitudes, as men often do in handling types, parables, and similitudes. As a string overstretched makes jarring disharmony, such a practice shows more fondness than soundness.

1. The Paschal lamb must be a male lamb without blemish, the son of the first year taken from the sheep or goats (Exodus 12:5). And this resembles Christ Himself and His perfection. There were many blemishes which the superstitious or curious Jews observed, as many as 60 or 70; any blemish disabled a lamb. Christ was without all blemish. Nothing was excepted from other men, in His likeness to them, but sin. He was in all points tempted as we are, yet without sin. He was of masculine perfection, at the perfection of his age, about 33 or 34 years of age, of lamb-like humility and meekness, which are noted in Him as exemplary graces.

He was prefigured in the lamb of the daily sacrifice, in the lamb of the Passover, in Abraham's ram instead of Isaac, in the scapegoat (Leviticus 16:21), and pointed out by John the Baptist under this name: "Behold, the Lamb of God." It is implied (Hebrews 9:28) that He shall appear the second time apart from sin that in His first coming He was not without; but we must distinguish this sin (as being ours imputed to Him), and so He was made sin for us so as to bear it in His body, which at His second coming He shall not bear or be laden with as He was before. And therefore He is said to come without sin, both His and ours.

2. This Paschal lamb was to be separated from the flock and set apart for sacrifice on the tenth day of the month, but not killed till the fourteenth day in the evening, or, according to that vexed phrase, between the two evenings. In other words, the lamb was to be killed in the afternoon when the sun declined, but before sunset. And it was about that same time of day that our Savior, the true Passover, was slain. But in a further meaning it shows that Christ was set apart and foredesigned of God to be our Passover long before, not in His decree, but in His promise, and the predictions of the prophets which have been since the world began (Luke 1:70). "But now in the end of the world has He appeared to put away sin by the sacrifice of Himself" (Hebrews 9:26).

He suffered between the two evenings of the world, which was in His declination. When He came, that was our evening; and the latter is to come. The days of His appearance are often called "the last days." And though that has another meaning, showing the unalterableness of the gospel ordinances contrary to those of the law, yet we may affirm that it was past the noon of the world when He came, and the time shall not be so long after unto sunset as before.

3. This Paschal lamb must be killed, the blood taken into a barn sprinkled with hyssop. It shall be on every door, the flesh roasted with fire, not eaten

raw or boiled in water, the head, legs, and innards
(Exodus 12:7–9, 22). And this may set forth unto us
the unutterable sufferings of Christ, both in His
soul and body, which the Scripture sets out with
such an emphasis of words. I mean especially those
of His soul, scorched with the sense of God's extreme wrath, which are expressed by extraordinary
words: "sweating like drops of blood, with expression of strong cries and tears." O man, you understand not the sufferings of this Passover lamb
roasted with fire, forbidden to be boiled in scalding
water, for that does not express the sufferings in ex-
tremity. And what is all this for? To make Christ
more pleasant meat to you, which, if you feed upon,
and with a bunch of hyssop sprinkle this blood, ap-
plying it by faith, eating this roasted flesh and
drinking this blood poured forth, it will feast your
soul and secure you from the wrath of God, which is
the next point.

4. The destroying angel, seeing this blood on the
doorposts, passes over the house, goes and kills the
Egyptians' firstborn, and executes God's last plague
upon them. In the meantime the Israelites were safe
within the protection of blood (Exodus 12:12–13).
And here is the safety of those Israelites: believers
who have applied by faith the blood of Jesus Christ,
when God shall let loose His last and final plagues
upon the world, shall be safe; hell, wrath, and con-
demnation shall not touch them. "When I see the
blood," He said, "I'll pass over you" (Exodus 12:13,
23). Nothing else will save you. God looks at nothing but the blood of Christ upon you. Happy are they
who, before God rides His circuit of destruction to

make a cry in all Egypt, have gotten under the sanctuary of blood, for then the plague shall not be upon you when God smites the land of Egypt (Exodus 12:13).

5. After the Israelites had been secured from the stroke of that dismal night, then immediately they marched away and were begged by the Egyptians to be gone. Four hundred and thirty years they were enslaved, and God, being punctual in His times, finished their captivity in that hour and began to fulfill His promises which He had made to them about bringing them into their promised land (Exodus 12:31–33, 41–42). And here we see that when a soul has long lien in the base bondage of sin and the devil, and comes to take hold of Christ and is sprinkled with His blood, and enters into covenant with God in Christ, then he is set free from his bondage and goes out of Egypt. Then all the promises begin to open upon him and he sets upon his heavenly journey, and no Pharaoh can hinder him any longer. All the sweet promises of peace, comfort, and hope begin to be made good to him, for they are all "yea and amen in Christ."

The devil and all his power and instruments cannot hold him; the blood is upon him, and from that hour he is a free man to own no lord but God. And yet still he has a wilderness to go through, but he is miraculously carried as Israel was through it. But it must not be expected that they should eat the Passover and stay in Egypt still; they must go out of their bondage who are sprinkled with this blood of the covenant.

In a similar case, God said, "I have sent out thy

prisoners out of the pit wherein there is no water"
(Zechariah 9:11). Perhaps this type is yet to be fulfilled in the gospel churches whom the Lord will
deliver out of the hands of their oppressing tyrants,
be it Pope or Turk—not by the sword, but by ordinances of His covenant. And then, if they shall pur-
sue a people under blood, as Pharaoh did, there will
be a red sea to swallow them, horse and man.

And so much for the Passover as referring to
Christ our Sacrifice, for that it does so is plain by
this: that which is said of the Paschal lamb in
Exodus 12:46 is expressly applied to and fulfilled in
Christ in John 19:36. So much for the Passover as a
sacrifice, or as the figure of our sacrifice and theirs,
Christ Jesus.

The Lord's Supper Considered as a Sacrament

Now we proceed to consider it as a sacrament,
not ours, but theirs; nor yet a figure of our sacrament in propriety, though often so called in transit,
and much contended for by papists. For what Jew
could ever have seen our Supper prefigured in that
Passover? And in what propriety can our sacrament
be the sacrament of another. Christ is the substance
of the sacrament, both theirs and ours. There they
meet as the inward circumcision and regeneration
is the essence of their circumcision and our baptism, but that one sacrament should be the figure of
another is absurd and void of reason. As two pictures
of one man are both resemblances of that one man,
but one is not the picture of another, similarly, because the Passover has the common nature of a

sacrament, it points to the same Christ as our Supper. And from that the Apostle draws an argument from to persuade gospel Christians to holiness. Therefore we shall consider what significance there is in it, for though the signs are not ours, yet the significance is.

1. The Passover or Paschal lamb, as killed and roasted and the blood sprinkled, was a sacrifice; as eaten by the Israelites and feasted upon, it was a sacrament. And in later times, both by Jewish records and by Scripture, it appears (2 Chronicles 35:11 and Ezra 6:20) that the Levites killed the Paschals, the priests sprinkled the blood on the altar, and then they took the lamb to their families or chambers in Jerusalem, and there ate it.

So in our Supper, there is a sacrifice slain and offered up for atonement, and that is Christ's body and blood. And then there is an eating and drinking of this sacrifice in the sacrament of bread and wine, as in many sacrifices of the law there was first an offering up to God and then a feasting on the remainder. We have a true sacrifice, Christ, offered up to God for us. We have a true sacrament, as that sacrifice is eaten and drunk by us. The oblation belongs to God to propitiate and redeem; the communication belongs to us to be refreshed and nourished. Their eating the Passover was no sacrifice but a sacrament; their killing and roasting the lamb made it eatable. Christ's sacrificing Himself for us renders Him fit nourishment for us. Had He not been a sacrifice offered up for us, what profit would there have been in eating and drinking sacramentally and spiritually that body and blood?

This consideration is of special remark: you feast upon a sacrifice; you feed upon a sacrifice. The mouth eats the sacrament; the eye of faith discerns the sacrifice. The sacrament is no sacrifice, but the commemoration and communication of a sacrifice. And here it must be observed why God instituted their Passover and our answerable sacrament to consist of meat and drink, eating and drinking. I conceive that it was the most proper way to partake of a sacrifice; for how else can it be? Therefore we eat and drink by way of preparation of our sacrifice. Hence the phrase "living upon the altar, eating of the altar" (Hebrews 13:10). And thus, if we carry our eye to the earthly part in the Supper, and to the heavenly part, that is to the sacrament and the sacrifice represented, and feed upon the sacrifice represented as well as the sacrament it represents, we then "discern the Lord's body."

2. Their Passover was instituted as an ordinance forever, for a memorial of their deliverance in Egypt and their education out of it. It was a commemoration to be observed forever, that is, in all succeeding generations as long as their polity and religion stood (Exodus 12:14, 24, 42). And we read about some of this in Jewish writers.

What do you mean by this service, that in every company of Passover communicants there was someone who rehearsed and made commemoration, the history of the Passover? God would have the sacrifice of Christ for our sin, that greatest work of His, and our deliverance thereby from worse than Egypt or a destroying angel, to be observed and kept in mind by a lasting trophy or monument, our

Supper. The Apostle, in alluding to their custom, uses a word in 1 Corinthians 11:26 ("as often as ye eat this bread and drink this cup, ye do show forth the Lord's death till He come") that means "to commemorate," or "with thanksgiving and affection to set it forth." And as theirs was forever till Christ's first coming, so ours is forever till His second coming. As long as their church continued they were charged with this ordinance. As long as the gospel church continues, we are charged with this ordinance; and therefore neither the doctrine of the gospel nor the doctrine of the sacraments shall anyone remove or alter till Christ comes.

3. Their Passover in Egypt was eaten in their various families or societies, a lamb per house, except if it was too little (Exodus 12:3–4); and in later times when this was repealed (Deuteronomy 16:6–7), and was confined to the place that God would choose, and so to Jerusalem, then, though the lamb might be slain in the holy court and the blood sprinkled on the altar, yet they carried it home to their hired chambers and there ate in companies, not less than ten in a fraternity, nor above twenty, but never a man alone. Though Christ is our sacrifice, once offered upon the cross as a sacrifice to God, yet our Supper brings Him home to us into our churches and into our souls. There an application of Him is to be made, the blood sprinkled on our doors, and the Paschal brought home to our own house. "Take ye, eat ye, drink ye."

God comes to particulars with us, and the application of the sacrifice is the life of the sacrament. We must eat and drink at home in our own souls.

Christ comes home to us, and yet this Supper ought, like the Passover, to be eaten in societies. I know no reason for one to eat it alone. There must be a company, for it is a communion. One person does not make a communion. The Apostle said, "When you come into a meeting, when you come together, tarry for one another" (1 Corinthians 11:20, 33–34). Hence it has been anciently called "a meeting, a congregation." Arthur Hildersham, in his commentary on John 4, said, "It's God's ordinance that the Lord's Supper be administered in public assemblies. How can there be a communicant without a communion? Not that the walls of a church make it a communion, but a meeting of believers."

4. Their Passover was eaten with unleavened bread and sour or bitter herbs (Exodus 12:8). There are many circumstances and ceremonies found in the Jewish authors about the searching out of all leaven, yea, with candles at noonday, and an execration of all leaven if any should remain unsound, and the bitter herbs were in constant use. The unleavened bread reminded them in what haste they went out of Egypt (Exodus 12:33), and the bitter herbs what affliction and bondage they had suffered, and further than that they did not see.

The Apostle interprets leaven as malice and wickedness, and unleavened bread as sincerity and truth (1 Corinthians 5:8), and so it teaches us how Christ is to be received by us, and what manner of persons we ought to be who apply and receive Jesus Christ. We must remember our bondage under sin, not with delight, but bitterness, and feel the sour taste of our former ways, as contrite and broken sinners. Bitter herbs are good sauce for the Paschal Lamb. Sin felt sets an edge on the stomach like vinegar. Christ relishes well to such a soul.

When you come to eat His Supper, bring your own sauce with you, bitter herbs, and refresh yourself on the memory of your old ways and former lusts. That's the sauce; the bread is unleavened bread. You cannot eat the lamb and leaven together, as a secure hypocrite, a filthy swine not purged from sin. You cannot think to have Christ and your sin too, to be pardoned and not purged, to be saved and not sanctified. Away, and never think to eat this Lamb with leavened bread. You may come with bitter herbs, with contrition for sin, but you may not come with and in your sins, for that's eating with leavened bread. Therefore, search it out and let your sins be searched out as with a candle, and let them be execrable to you so that God may see your hatred *of* them and your loathing of yourself *for* them.

5. Their Passover in Egypt was to be eaten with loins girded, with shoes on feet, and with staff in hand. They were to eat in haste (Exodus 12:11), and therefore standing as ready to be instantly on their march to leave the land of Egypt and go seek their promised country. This signifies to us that we must receive Christ and His blood with intent and purpose to leave the dominion of Pharaoh, the kingdom, service, and bondage of sin, and the devil. And from that hour we are to set forward towards our heavenly country. This is that hard doctrine of the gospel. This makes men neglect and refuse Jesus Christ, because they cannot part with sin. They will not resolve to quit the former course, just as the man

who "went away sorrowful, for he had great posses-
sions." So men will not be saved, but will go away
sorrowfully, for they have powerful, pleasing, and
profitable lusts. And, as it may allude to our Supper,
let it teach us to come to the table of the Lord with
staves in our hands and our loins girded up, like
men resolving to march and begin a new and holy
life. "Henceforth we should not serve sin" (Romans
6:6).

6. In their Passover, they had to eat and roast a
whole lamb, and nothing of it was to remain till the
morning. If any did remain, it had to be burned with
fire (Exodus 12:9–10), the flesh was to be eaten, and
not a bone of it broken (Numbers 9:12). This shows
that Christ is all meat. There is no waste in Him.
There is a variety of nourishment for all our uses—
righteousness, peace, comfort, and contentment to
fill our capacities, relieve our temptations, pardon
and purge away our sins. We must not divide Him,
but take Him whole—His merit and Spirit, His salvation and sovereignty. Christ is our Way, our Truth,
and our Life.

What an unhappy doctrine is that of the papists
who take the blood from us and will not let the people drink! It is as if they should not allow our
Passover to be a whole lamb. And just as unhappy are
they who not only rend His coat, but break His
bones by depraving the fundamentals of gospel doctrine and tearing the Creed article from article until
nothing is left, for in the morning light of the
gospel all those shadows shall be abolished and dis-
claimed. Rivet says that sacraments are not sacraments except in their use, and only while they are

used, as the bread and wine after their use are not sacraments. A mere stone is a boundary in its place; remove it and it is a stone, not a marker.

7. No uncircumcised person may eat the Passover (Exodus 12:44, 48), nor any unclean person (Numbers 9:7), where the instance is of one made unclean by the dead, but it extended to other uncleannesses, such as a leprous or menstruous person. Yet there was provision made for the unclean that they might keep the Passover in the second month, as they did in Hezekiah's Passover (2 Chronicles 30:13). But for the uncircumcised there was no provision, and this sets forth to us two sorts of men who are incapable of worthily coming to the Lord's Supper:

(1) The uncircumcised who are strangers and foreigners to the church, and who are not initiated by the first sacrament of baptism. No person of whatever condition who is unbaptized can come to the Supper, for he is not entered and admitted into church fellowship or communion by the first sacrament. He is not one of the house or of the fraternity where the lamb is eaten, and out of the house the Passover must not be carried. Those who are out of the church have no right to the privileges of the church, just as those who are not freemen have not the privileges of the city. It was never known in the old church that an uncircumcised person, nor in the gospel church that an unbaptized person partook of either of the suppers, theirs or ours, for both of them are second sacraments, not first. The way to the Table has ever been by the font or laver of washing.

(2) The domestics of the house who were circumcised Israelites, yet if they at the time of the Passover were unclean, were not to eat it. This case came into question when some who were unclean put the case to Moses. He delayed the decision till he had asked of the Lord, and the Lord judged that he should be put off to the Passover of the second month. And this tells us, by way of allusion, that a baptized member of the church, yea, a true believer, may be unfit at some particular time to come to the Lord's Table and may eat and drink unworthily. Were not the Corinthians such men and in such a case (1 Corinthians 11)? Were they not punished for their unworthy coming, even though, doubtless, some of them were godly and all professing Christians?

8. There were in the first Passover in Egypt, used and commanded by expressed words, certain rituals for that occasion only which, as Jewish writers and practice show, were omitted and not used in later times. These included eating in dispersed houses, but later in Jerusalem only; the taking up the lamb four days before, which we read not of afterwards; the striking of the doorposts with blood; not going out of the house that night, which in later times Christ and His disciples did; eating in traveling posture with staves, whereas we find that our Savior, and the Jews, in another posture of discumbrance, ate lying on beds. These, or at least some of these, were occasional at first, and, the occasion ceasing, custom ruled otherwise without offense.

In our Supper the Lord celebrated and instituted it at night, in or at the end of the Paschal and com-

mon supper. He used unleavened bread. It was late at
night. He was in a gesture of leaning or lying down
(John 13:25). It was in the chamber of a private
house. There was no woman present. He blessed and
consecrated the bread and wine apart. They sang a
hymn at the close of all, as was usual. And these, or
many of these, were occasional circumstances by
reason of the custom and rite of the Paschal supper,
or the particular exigency of the time.

And what, then? Do they oblige to a hair's
breadth all later ages? Do those who impose any one
of these themselves hold to all of them? Shall we be
supercilious and superstitious in observing all occasional or local customs? Why do we not appear in
sackcloth at our feasts? As the Apostle said about the
length of hair, so I say, "If any man seem to be con-
tentious, we have no such custom, nor the churches
of God." If Christ had celebrated the Supper with His
loins girded and staff in hand, we would not have
been bound to it. Yet we must not follow this freedom too far, and, under color of disregarding an
occasional circumstance, change or mutilate the
real substance, as the Papist does who takes away the
cup which Christ blessed and breaks not the bread
as He did, and who, of a sacrament, makes a sacrifice. The matter and form, the intended analogy between the sign and the thing signified, will guide us
in our distinguishing substance from incidental
features.

The Lord's Supper Is a Federal Ordinance

Implying a Covenant Transaction between God and Us, and Supposing a Renewal of Solemn Vows to be the Lord's

by Edmund Calamy

We are often to renew with great solemnity the sacred memorials of our dearest Savior who gave His life as a ransom for us, and sealed with His blood that covenant of grace and peace that is between God and us. Our vow in baptism indeed binds us fast to God, and our owning its obligation on us tends to increase its force. Yet God thinks it fit to require and take new security of us, and orders us to come to His table that we may there strengthen our obligations, and not only own again and again that we are His by right, but be guided by the awful and affecting considerations there presented to us to new resolutions and engagements and solemn vows to lead a life of holy devotedness. And in requiring this of us, He very much considers our benefit.

That I may handle this matter to the best advantage, I will:

1. Make it appear that the Lord's Supper is a federal ordinance, that it naturally implies a covenant transaction between God and us, and therefore supposes renewed vows on our part—vows being ever an

essential part of such transactions.

2. Show that the more expressly the Christian vow is renewed by us every time we come to the Lord's Table, the more effectually and plentifully we are likely to reap the benefits of that ordinance.

3. Give some directions for the right management of the renewal of our vows at such a time, and endeavor to give some help in reducing this matter to practice.

The first of these particulars is the subject of this chapter; the other two of the next.

The Lord's Supper is, in its own nature, a federal ordinance, which implies a covenant transaction between God and us and supposes a renewal of our vows to be the Lord's. This is that which I am now to discuss, to which undertaking I am the more inclined because I imagine there are multitudes who sit down time after time at the Lord's Table who don't sufficiently consider this matter. They look on that sacred festival as an ordinance instituted to keep up the remembrance of Christ and what He has done and suffered for the recovery of a lost world, and therefore, when they come to it, they endeavor to think affectionately of His incarnation, passion, and crucifixion; and thus far indeed 'tis well. But when they stop here and go no further, they leave out a main thing, which lies in that covenant transaction between their God and Savior and them, which is thereby designed.

Withal, there are many others who indeed look on themselves as obliged to renew their covenant and repeat their solemn vows every time they come to this ordinance, who yet know not why they are obliged to it then any more than at another time. They know not on what to base this apprehension of theirs, which they have received from others and take for granted without any examination of its grounds. I shall therefore, from the following considerations, make it appear that a renewed covenanting is one aspect of this ordinance necessary to be taken into account by those who would rightly conceive of it; and that 'tis not without cause that persons are ordinarily pressed hereto.

First, therefore, consider the mutual action in this ordinance of giving and taking between God and us, and you will see plain evidence in the nature of the thing of a covenant transaction. Giving and taking are the first obvious actions in this solemnity. Giving is God's part and taking is ours. God gives us bread and wine by His delegated officer; we receive them from the minister as from His representative. Now, pray consider a little what it is that is given and taken at that time. "'Tis plain, simple bread and wine," you'll say. And 'tis true, no more falls under the view of sense. But what is it that is thereby signified? Is it not a bruised, nay, a broken Christ, giving His soul as an offering for sin, and shedding His blood to make atonement? 'Tis Christ with all His benefits that there is given to the believing soul.

As certainly as bread and wine are put into the devout communicant's hands, so certainly is he invested in all gospel benefits. God gives Himself, His Son, His Spirit, His grace, His favor, and all that can be reasonably desired or truly wanted to the believing soul. This is on one side.

On the other side, the believer takes. With his hands he takes the distributed bread and wine, and receives with all his heart what is thereby portrayed and represented. He receives an offered Christ in his arms and into his heart. In short, God actually makes over, makes a delivery, as it were, of all that He promises in the covenant of grace on His part. We, by taking then what He gives, naturally engage to all that in that covenant He has made our duty. This is the more evident in that a firm disposition and bent of heart, to the performance of all such duty, is a prerequisite to the actual conveyance of those benefits.

Further, we may observe how customary it has been, and is among men, by giving and taking the smallest things to ratify compacts of the greatest consequence. A man may among us give away all he has by the delivery of a flagon, which custom considered may answer the objection which the appearing meanness of the things given and taken at the Lord's Supper, compared with the great things thereby represented and made over, might give occasion to. The giving and taking but of sixpence to strike up a contract lays as fast hold of a man as ten thousand pounds in hand. Much more, then, does this solemn giving and taking of bread and wine, which Christ has made a part of His religion, and whereby He is so closely represented, bind us as fast to Him as if we should repeat every word that He has said and profess our hearty consent unto it.

Observe further under what notion Christ is given at that ordinance to every truly hungering and thirsting soul. "Behold," says God there to all such persons, "here's a Christ for you, to be taken by you, as your Prophet, Priest, and King." Whereto the prepared soul naturally replies, "Lord, I am ready to take Him as Thou offerest Him to me. I'm for a whole Christ, in all the parts of His saving office. I'll take Him for my Prophet, and credit Him in all things; for my Priest, and in Him I'll put all my trust; and for my King, to whom, Thy grace enabling me, I'll yield a sincere, preserving obedience." This is plainly a renewed covenant, a short summary of the Christian vow.

Second, consider also the actions of eating and drinking, and you'll see further evidence of a covenant transaction. At this holy Supper we come to eat and drink with the blessed God. He is indeed invisible to us, but has designated one in each Christian assembly to represent Him, and in His name and stead to entertain those who come to Him as His guests. He spreads a table, and provides us food so that, eating and drinking, we may receive nourishment for our spiritual life and supports for our spiritual welfare. Now, eating and drinking and feasting together, we may observe in Scripture history, were the usual appendages of compacts or covenants, as we may see in Genesis 26:30 and 31:44–46, where we find Isaac and Abimelech, Jacob and Laban concluding their compacts with a feast.

The same is evident in many other places. The eating and drinking together of those who were at variance implies an antecedent agreement, for it is a token of friendly familiarity not wont to be afforded to enemies. Abimelech hated Isaac, and would not have eaten and drunk with him, but upon supposition they were agreed. Nor would Laban have done the like with Jacob, whom he pursued with a design of destruction, but upon the same supposition. It is an axiom in the civil law that if anyone does but drink to another against whom he has an accusation of slander or other verbal injury, he loses his action because he is now assumed to be reconciled to him. The Hebrew word that signifies a covenant, or any federal communion between parties, is derived from another word that signifies "to eat," because it was the constant custom of the Hebrews, and other oriental nations, to establish covenant by eating and drinking together.

Now by nature there is a great variance between God and us on account of our hereditary apostasy: Sin, as it sets us against God, so it sets Him against us. Where sin therefore reigns and bears sway, it is plain there is a great unfitness for eating and drinking with God at His table. That is a solemnity that supposes a person's peace first to be made with God through Christ; otherwise he is not likely to be a welcome guest. But even where a person's peace is actually made, there are frequent falls for which there must be a renewed repentance; and God's admitting us from time to time to feast with Him at His table, notwithstanding our manifold failings and defects, is a sufficient argument of His readiness to pass them by and to be reconciled anew. Whenever therefore we come to eat and drink with Him, we are to renew our self-dedication. There's none, not even the best, but what between one sacrament and another do enough to forfeit all their interest in the divine favor, were God so severe as to mark iniquity. Eating and drinking, therefore, with God after such renewed offenses supposes us anew to make our peace with Him, to devote ourselves to Him afresh, as ever we would keep His favor; for which we at no time have such an advantage as at His Table.

This will be further evident from a third consideration, which is taken from that which we feast upon at the Lord's Table: the memorials of the great Christian sacrifice. The most general and proper notion of the Lord's Supper, the notion to which all that relates to it may very aptly be referred, is this: It is a solemn feast upon the memorials of the sacrifice of infinite virtue that was offered by our Savior upon the cross for sin (this is excellently explained by the learned Dr. Cudworth), which notion is too large to be here distinctly handled, and therefore I shall meddle with no more of it than what concerns my present purpose. It is easy to observe how commonly covenants between God and man were attended with sacrifices. Thus it was in Noah's case; 'twas the same in Abraham's case (Genesis 8–9 and 15). So also sacrifices accompanied the covenant God entered into with the Israelites all in a body (Exodus 24:5, 8), and by such sacrifices offered the covenants made were confirmed.

It may be further observed that sacrifices were founded upon a covenant. The covenant God entered into with the Jews required them to offer up the several sacrifices prescribed in the Law, which, had they not been founded on a divine covenant, would have been in no way likely to have been accepted. But suppose the covenant once settled that required them, and the sacrifices now appear to have been federal rites; they were memorials of the covenant between God and the people—memorials to God, putting Him in mind of His promises, and memorials to the people, putting them in mind of, and engaging and quickening them to, their duty. Each sacrifice offered implied a covenant transaction between God and him who made the oblation, which points to the true meaning of the passage which some have esteemed so difficult: "Gather My saints together that have made a covenant with Me by sacrifice" (Psalm 50:5), for sacrifices were appointed to be signs and seals of the covenant between God and His people. To this our blessed Lord seems to allude when, at the institution of the Supper, He says, "This cup is the new testament in My blood," which is to say, "Covenants were of old ratified by sacrifices, the blood of the sinner being originally required by the Law, but the offering being of the blood of another creature. But I pour out my own blood for you, and behold I now give it to you. It is therefore a new covenant, because it is not sealed with the blood of victims, but My own blood." This is also intimated by the apostle, when he says, "Not by the blood of goats and calves, but by His own blood, He entered into the holy place; and for this cause He is the Mediator of the new testament."

It may be further observed that as sacrifices were heretofore seals of the covenant, so eating the sacrifices was a proper appendix of most of their oblations. They had four sorts of sacrifices in use among them: burnt offerings, sin offerings, trespass offerings, and peace offerings. Burnt offerings were wholly offered up to God and consumed on the altar, neither priests nor people having therein any part or portion. In sin offerings and trespass offerings God had a part consumed on His altar, and the priests a part to eat of. They ate of them as the people's proxies, being mediators with God for those who, by bringing an oblation for a sin or trespass, were supposed to be sensible of a defilement. But of their peace offerings, as God had a part and the priests a part, so they themselves also who brought them had a part, of which they might eat together with their friends, feasting and rejoicing before the Lord.

We have in the Old Testament divers instances of persons feasting before the Lord on these sacrifices that were called peace offerings. Thus we find Moses and Aaron and all the elders of Israel offering sacrifices, and feasting upon them before God when they were done (Exodus 18:12). So also at the general covenant before mentioned, many sacrifices being offered, we find they ate and drank and saw the Lord, and upon the nobles of the children of Israel He laid not His hand (Exodus 24:11). Again we find Elkanah making a yearly journey to the holy city (1 Samuel 1:3–4) to offer sacrifices, and to feast upon them with his family before the Lord. Many other passages are of the same nature, but it is needless to mention them.

It may be further observed that eating God's sacrifices was a federal rite between God and those who offered them. For God, designing to have a peculiar residence among the Jews, resolved to live, as it were, in a regal state among them, and therefore the tem-

ple was His palace, the priests and Levites His guard
and attendants. His house had its several apartments
for several offices, with furniture suited thereto. On
the altar was His fire, which was never to go out, and
the sacrifices offered were His provision. Not that
He could really eat the flesh of bulls and drink the
blood of goats (Psalm 50:13)—as He upbraids those
who were apt to rest in externals—but by these
things and their allusive significations He served
sundry wise and great ends and purposes. Now sacrifices then passing under the notion of God's provision, it was a mark of great favor to be admitted to
partake of them. And sacrifices being seals of the
covenant, feasting upon the remainders of them was
a further engagement to those who offered them to
fulfill their part of the covenant with God, by whom,
by their being admitted to feast with Him, they had
reason to hope they were accepted.

Let not any think all this a digression, as such
thoughts and reflections as these may be of use in
helping us to understand these matters, without
some light in which (and in others of the like nature) we must necessarily be in the dark when we are
reading the greatest part of the Old Testament.
Besides this, I say, these remarks are all to my present purpose because of the resemblance these
things carry in them to those that I am now upon.
For as sacred covenants were heretofore attended
with sacrifices, so the covenant between God and us,
that covenant on which all our hopes are founded,
is attended with and confirmed by the sacrifice of
our Savior, which at His table we commemorate. As
their sacrifices were federal rites, and signs and

seals of the covenant between God and the people, so is our solemn commemoration of the sacrifice once offered for us on the cross a federal rite. And this sacred institution is a sign and seal of the covenant between God and us, founded in the blood of our dearest Savior. And as they were then to make a covenant with God by sacrifice, so are we now to confirm our covenant with Him over the memorials of our great gospel sacrifice.

Further, as the Jewish feasts were upon the flesh of the sacrifices they offered to God, so is our holy Supper a feast upon the sacrifice which Christ once offered for us. And as their feasts upon their sacrifices were federal rites and bands of federal communion between God and them, so the Lord's Supper, which is also a feast upon a sacrifice, must be a federal feast between God and us, whereby, eating and drinking at His own table and partaking of His meat, we are taken into a sacred covenant and inviolable league of friendship with Him. As God, by those sacrifices and the feasts upon them, ratified His covenant with those who partook of them, inasmuch as they did, in a manner, eat and drink with Him, so He confirms His covenant with us by the sacred symbols at His table of which He allows us to partake. And as the people, by feasting on those sacrifices with God, ratified and confirmed the covenant on their part, so we, by feasting on this sacrifice, ratify and confirm the covenant between God and us.

As a third point, as the Jews joined themselves to God by feasting in His house on His sacrifices, so we join ourselves to Christ by feasting in the place of

His worship, at His table, upon the memorials of His body and blood. And our obligations to stick to Him, to follow and obey Him, as much exceed all other ties, in their sacredness, strength, and virtue, as the sacrifice of Christ surpasses that of a beast, or as the eating and drinking of His body and blood is beyond all participation in the meat of the ancient altars. There being therefore in the Lord's Supper so plain a representation of a sacrifice, which ever had a relation to a covenant, and it being a feasting upon the memorials of this sacrifice, which feasting was ever a federal rite, this must be a federal ordinance.

Add hereto, fourth, the consideration of the admonition which naturally seems to be implied in this ordinance. Our Lord is, at His table, represented in our view as a sacrifice for sin, enduring the utmost torments, miseries, and sorrows for our sakes, all which have a loud voice to us. He seems, as it were, at His table to adjure every one by His agonies and conflicts, by His blood and wounds, by His cross and passion, by all that He underwent for their sakes, to love Him and be faithful to Him; to hate and fly from sin and renounce the devil and all his works, lest they, as much as in them lies, undo what He has been doing, crucify Him afresh, and renew His pain. Those therefore who, after this, lay their hands on the memorials of the broken, bleeding body of Christ do, as it were, call heaven and earth to witness that they will ever live to Him who died for them, and rather die than renounce His service.

Now the very heathens reckoned that a vow or oath made when persons laid their hands on the warm entrails of a beast (which was upon occasion customary with them) was the most solemn oath that could be made. How much more solemn, then, should we esteem vows made when we lay our hands on the memorials of the sacred body of Christ!

Fifth, and last, it has been the sense of all Christians from the first ages to the present day that the Lord's Supper is a federal ordinance; which is a consideration of no small weight in a matter of this nature. Among many evidences that might be given hereof I shall mention but two.

The primitive Christians so sacredly and solemnly bound themselves by vows at the Lord's Supper to their God and Savior that the heathens were ready to suspect them of dangerous plots and conspiracies. While Pliny the Younger, a learned heathen, candidly endeavors to acquit them from this charge, at the same time he gives us an account of some of the vows they renewed at this ordinance every time. "They assemble themselves (says he in a letter to Trajan the Emperor, still extant) before daybreak, and sing a hymn to Christ as if He were God, and then bind themselves with a sacrament or oath, not to do mischief to any, that they will not rob or steal or commit adultery, nor falsify their words, nor deny their trust, and the like. And then, after they have eaten together, they depart to their own homes." But though his account is made up of negatives, we may be well satisfied they added positive vows to them.

My other evidence is taken from the name of "sacrament," which they gave to this ordinance jointly with that of baptism. The word "sacrament" is

nowhere to be found in Scripture, but is plainly of
human origin; and it was used very early in the
Church to express and signify those two ordinances
of baptism and the Lord's Supper. In the process of
time it was also applied to other things. Now the
word "sacrament" properly signifies an oath. It was
originally the military oath which the soldiers took
when they swore fidelity to their emperors. When
therefore we find this term of "sacrament" applied
by Christians in the first ages to the Lord's Supper,
and used ever since to express it, it implies that they
have all been sensible that it was a federal ordinance, since the word they use for it intimates that
we in that ordinance come under an oath to Christ,
much like the oath of fidelity which the soldiers
took to their emperors. And indeed, if we would acquit ourselves rightly, every time we come to the
Lord's table, we must vow and engage that we'll
continue as Christ's faithful servants, subjects, and
soldiers, and never do anything against His crown
and dignity as long as we live.

Let us, then, reflect a little and pause. Let us
think how strange an instance it is of condescen-
sion by the great Majesty of heaven that He should
vouchsafe to hold any federal communion with such
as we are, with us sinners, who have so much pro-
voked Him as to deserve to be utterly abandoned by
Him; with us sinners of the Gentiles who were once
without God and without Christ, and strangers to
the covenant of promise; that God should suffer us
to lay hold of His covenant, that He should admit us
to feast with Him upon the signs and seals of it, admit us to such a relationship of familiarity, and ad-

vance us to such an honor, which is at the same time so much for our benefit, comfort, and security. Oh, bless the Lord and magnify His name! Exalt Him highly and show forth His praise, who disdains not to regard us, though we are low and mean and vile and despicable; nay, who treats us poor mortals, time after time, as if we were a sort of angels, admitting us to feast and rejoice with Him in our commemoration of His love and renewal of His covenant.

Let's think withal, and that seriously, of His great kindness to us in multiplying ties and bonds upon us, that He may more effectually engage us to Himself. Our God is sensible of the slipperiness of our hearts, and therefore He is for binding us as fast as may be. He has so ordered matters that we are to be consecrated and come under a vow to Him as soon almost as we begin to be. This vow we are, with great solemnity, to own and renew as soon as we become capable of transacting for ourselves; and afterwards we are required frequently to give new security of our fidelity over the consecrated elements at the Supper of our Lord. And the design of all is only the more effectually to engage us to that which is our unquestionable duty, wherewith our interest is closely connected. In obliging us time after time to renew our bonds, God has considered our good, designing thereby to further our security of reaching those inestimable benefits which He has designed for us. We should therefore, so far from thinking these bonds onerous, prize them; we should look upon ourselves as so much the more honored by how much more they are multiplied upon us.

The Express Renewal of Our Christian Vows

*Every Time We Come to the Holy Communion,
and Directions about the Right
Management of It*

by Edmund Calamy

It now follows that, in the second place, I show how the express renewal of the Christian vow, every time we come to the Supper of our Lord, will help us more effectually to reap the benefits of that holy ordinance. This comes in very properly by way of motive to that which I fear is too commonly neglected by many Christians: expressly renewed covenants at every sacrament. What I have to propound under this head will, I say, properly come by way of motive, for if I can make it appear that this is the way for us to reach the benefits designed for us by this sacred institution of religion, I think there are none who are not their own enemies but must readily fall in with it and set themselves to put it in practice. It is indeed certain and undeniable that a believer's growth in grace and advancement in the divine life may be promoted by their devout partaking of the holy Supper, while yet, either through ignorance, forgetfulness, or unskillfulness how to manage themselves at the sacred solemnity, they may neglect the express renewing of their vows to be the Lord's.

But if it is evident that this ordinance would do them more good, and be attended with much greater advantage to the same persons, if they positively and expressly every time made an act of surrender of themselves to Him who gave Himself for them, and anew engaged to live to Him who died for them, it will follow that they must be enemies to themselves if they continue negligent. Now this will be made to appear from these three considerations: (1) our slippery hearts will be more fixed and awed; (2) our faith and hope will be more confirmed and strengthened; and (3) our comfort will be more increased by this means than could be otherwise be supposed.

1. The express renewing of our vows every time we come to the Lord's table will much fix and awe our slippery hearts. None can be ignorant of how apt our hearts are to turn aside like a deceitful bow, and to lose the sense of those things which ought continually to influence and govern us, especially if removed from us by any distance of time; how easily the continually surrounding objects of sense deface those impressions which are at any time made on our minds by higher things; and how difficult it is to keep worldly engagements from prevailing over spiritual ones. Alas, the sensual, carnal part is so powerful in the best persons, and our hearts are so apt to fall in with it, and the temptations we meet with to draw off our hearts from God are so numerous, and we are so prone to yield unto them, that we can hardly tie ourselves fast enough, or sufficiently multiply obligations on ourselves to a holy, Christian, and divine life. If the sense of oft-repeated

engagements is apt to wear off (and who sees not that it too often does so even in the best?), how unlikely is it that a single act of consecrating ourselves to our God and Savior, or the same act repeated only now and then after large and considerable intervals, should retain a constant governing power over us!

But the frequency and expressness of our renewed vows (if we but take care to apply ourselves to them with any degree of that seriousness that suits such a solemnity) will much promote their influence upon us; for it will keep us under a standing sense of our obligation. It will fortify us against temptations; it will be a constant fence, spur, and monitor to us. For if I have the least degree of grace, and resolve not in the most daring and provoking manner possible to trifle with God and my own conscience; can I, while I am feasting on the memorials of redeeming love month after month, not help but renew my self-dedication to the Most High? Can I presently forget that I am another's and not my own? Can I or anyone so easily forget, as if it were but once or twice in a whole life's space, that solemn vows were made? And does not their expressness as well as their frequency add to their force? For this implies not only a recollection that we are the Lord's, but a serious resolution taken up in His presence, and formed over the most awful emblems of His greatness and majesty and purity, and the most endearing pledges of His goodness, grace, and love, that we will be His for the future more than ever we were before.

If we are serious in such frequently repeated engagements, we cannot but be made more watchful, more considerate and provident, more diligent, and more settled Christians, both in our tempers and lives, than we should otherwise be. Conscience's work will be made more easy, for we shall have but a little way at any time to look back to that which, of anything that can be thought of, will be the most likely to curb the fury of lust, abate the violence of temptation, quicken us to our duty, and cause repentance and rising again after our sins and falls. Now this is one of the blessed benefits designed for us by the institution of the sacrament of the Supper; it is more likely to be gained in no other way than by this practice of expressly renewing the Christian vow every time we join therein.

2. This practice will help to strengthen our faith and hope. There's no grace that is more employed at the sacrament by devout communicants than faith. Its work is to view Christ through the elements whereby He is represented, to receive Him when offered, and to return our all back to Him again— though not by way of requital, or out of any hope of reward, yet out of a sense of duty, and as a token of the highest gratitude.

A further office of the same grace is to behold the Father's mind and heart in that amazing mirror of His love that is there set before us, and to behold the divine Spirit in all His sanctifying gifts and graces, poured forth on all truly covenanting believers as the fruit of Christ's purchase, and to yield up the soul to be transformed into the same image by the same Spirit.

Nowhere has faith such an advantage for this work as at holy communion; and never is this advantage so well improved there as when our vows are seriously and expressly renewed, for thereby we show that the discoveries made by faith at that ordinance truly affect us and rightly work upon us. Thereby is our faith approved of the right stamp; and thereby is it made a governing principle of our tempers and lives. Withal, it is observable how express God is at His table as to all the several marks of His favor and love, which He makes over to us and bestows on us. These are received by faith. Certainly, therefore, it behooves us to be as express in our responses to Him. And hereby will our faith be strengthened by reason of the correspondence of our carriage in this respect towards God to His dealing with us, and also by reason of that riveted sense of faith's transactions at this ordinance that will be hereby occasioned.

Our hope also will hereby be strengthened—our hope of the acceptance of what we do, and of assistance in what we need, our hope of grace here and glory hereafter. The more express (if serious) anyone is in giving himself up to God at His table every time he comes there, the more reason he has to hope that God accepts him who never rejects a self-resigning soul; the more reason to hope for all the blessed fruits of the sacrifice and death of Christ, to whom he consecrated himself; the more reason to hope for all needed guidance and assistance from the blessed Spirit of grace, under whose conduct he freely puts himself; the more reason to hope for all he can need either in this world or another, since he so entirely commits himself to, and reposes his trust in, Him who is a suitable portion for him in either world.

3. Further (this follows upon the former), this practice will increase our comfort, which is one great design of the sacrament to promote. 'Tis indeed much to our comfort to be treated at so noble and costly a feast as God prepares for us when He spreads His table before us; 'tis comfortable to see what is there to be beheld, to receive what is offered, and to stand and take so delightful a prospect as we have there opportunity for. But the serious, express renewal of our vows to be the Lord's, and our solemn engagement to live as persons devoted to Him, are as great a spring of spiritual comfort as may be in all that ordinance. For this, according to the gospel message, lays a just foundation for a claim to all gospel blessings by virtue of the promises made through the blood we there commemorate. The holy communion implies an investiture in pardon and peace, reconciliation, adoption, and a right to eternal life, to all truly devout participants, to all who heartily devote themselves to their Lord and Redeemer.

Renewed vows, therefore, confirm our title to all both present and future blessings, and consequently lay a firm foundation for the highest comfort. For what can be more comfortable than for me, upon a review of what passed in that ordinance, to find that I am entitled to all those peculiar marks of divine favor which God in that ordinance makes over to His children, of which nothing can give greater assurance than our repeatedly devoting ourselves, with all the seriousness and solemnity we are able, to be His servants and subjects to our life's end? All these things taken together are, I think, abundantly sufficient to recommend this practice.

It yet remains that I give some directions about
this matter, and show how we should manage the
renewal of our vows to be the Lord's at the observance of every sacrament. Since this has been excellently done already by so many, I shall be but brief in
it. However, these eight following directions I can
recommend to any serious Christians.

Directions to Manage the Renewal of Our Vows

DIRECTION 1. *Before you go to renew your vows to be
the Lord's, recollect your past breaches, especially those since
your last solemn engagement.* Look not on this as an indifferent or inconsiderable matter, but as a thing
needful in order to dedicate yourselves anew to God
with any advantage. Take a convenient opportunity
for retiring from the world, and, when alone, set
yourselves down seriously to consider what strong
ties and bonds you are already under to be the
Lord's, and how little you answer them. Review your
lives; rip up your miscarriages; canvass all the secrets
of your hearts; endeavor to know the worst. For since
God knows all, 'tis in every way best that you should
do so too, that what is amiss may be rectified, and
His deserved displeasure averted. Consider your prevailing temper and stated tenor, and recollect your
demeanor upon particular occasions when you may
find reason to conclude the eye of God was most
upon you. Think how you have lived before the
blessed God, how you have behaved yourselves towards your Redeemer, and what has passed between
you and the Holy Spirit. Think how you have man-

aged yourselves in secret, in your families, and in your various relations; in your callings and business, and in your retirements; how you have carried it towards yourselves and others. Observe what corruptions you have most indulged, what temptations you have given way to, what neglects you have fallen into, and what positive guilt you have contracted. When time will allow it, running as far back in our lives as our memories will help us to do will be very proper and useful. And this should be done with more than ordinary carefulness at a person's first approach to the Lord's table. But when our confinements are greater, recollecting what has passed since the last sacrament may suffice, in which the more strict we are the better. Our eyes should particularly be on our Delilahs, whereby our affections are most entangled; and it should be a particular subject of inquiry as to what breaches of our last vows they have drawn us into. In general, let us lay our rule before us, and compare ourselves and our carriage with it, and that will soon reveal our defects. I need not tell a serious and considerate person the benefit of this practice.

DIRECTION 2. *Humble yourselves seriously before God for all past breaches with Him, whether known or unknown, before you offer to come under new vows to Him.* The more pains we take according to the foregoing direction, in searching and viewing ourselves, the more reason shall we find to cry out with the Psalmist, "Who can understand his errors? Cleanse Thou me from secret faults" (Psalm 19:12). For we have all some secret faults that we overlook. Therefore, I say, be humbled for all past breaches, known and unknown. Throw

yourselves at God's feet, and own your forfeitures of
His favor, and that you deserve His displeasure.
Abase yourselves out of a sense of your vileness, that
while you were engaged and pretended to live to
God, your Redeemer, you should have lived so much
to yourselves, so much to this present world, and so
much according to the dictates of your lusts. Be especially humbled for any particular failures that may
have had peculiarly aggravating circumstances at-
tending them. Think not of being accepted upon
the making of new vows while you are chargeable
with manifest breaches of your old ones that are un-
repented of. This humiliation and self-abasement,
with sorrow and shame for past breaches, is necessary by way of preparation in order that we may acceptably consecrate ourselves to God afresh.

DIRECTION 3. *Take heed of the extremes of levity and
over-great scrupulosity when you come to renew your vows at
the Lord's Table.* Take heed of levity, as if it were a
common, ordinary, and customary thing you were
setting yourselves about, when you go to give up
yourselves to God anew. This would be the way to
pull down a curse upon your heads instead of a
blessing. Beware therefore of rushing upon such sacred work with a common and unhallowed heart,
with a heart full of the world, with a heart prevail-
ingly addicted to any lust. On the other hand, also
beware of too great scrupulosity, in running matters
too high, as if unindulged infirmities and the want
of assurance were bars to acceptance, or as if perfection were necessary to obtaining the blessings of a
devoted state. This would be to pull yourself backward instead of advancing forward in the divine life.

Levity, in this case, is the effect either of habitual profaneness (than which nothing is more dreadful), of great negligence in preparatory work, or of gross ignorance of the nature, design, import, and solemnity of repeated—as well as initial—self-dedication. Overly-great scrupulosity, in this case, is sometimes the effect of a very timorous natural temper heightened by bodily indisposition, which makes persons the objects of compassion. At other times it arises from a mistake about the method of God's dealing with us under the new covenant dispensation, from a misunderstanding of the terms of the gospel, and too hard, sour, and severe thoughts of the blessed God unwarily imbibed. These errors of theirs, if they value their own peace or welfare, are carefully to be corrected. Though the former is generally the much more dangerous extreme of the two, yet the latter is very troublesome by reason that it will fill the soul with such fears as will exceedingly dampen and discompose it, and make it unfit for such work as the free, solemn, cheerful consecrating and devoting of oneself to God. Both, therefore, are, as much as in us lies, to be watched against.

DIRECTION 4. *Whenever we go to renew our vows to God, we should carefully mind with whom we are to transact, who we are who transact with Him, and for what purpose we do so.*

(1) We should remember with whom we transact, and to whom our vow is to be renewed: and that is, to God the Father, Son, and Spirit. God the Father, from whom we have apostatized, who yet is the Fountain of blessedness, in whom only we can be happy; God the Son, who is the only way to the

Father, our Mediator, Priest, Patron, Advocate, and
Helper; and God the Holy Spirit, who must be the
actual conveyor and introducer of all that light, life,
and love that shall capacitate us to enjoy the Father
through the Son, either in this or a better life. 'Tis
with the great God we in this affair have to do; 'tis to
Him whose majesty, glory, power, greatness, and
goodness are inconceivable and inexplicable that
we are, every time we come to the communion anew,
to give up ourselves. 'Tis with all three persons who
are called God that we in this affair are to transact.
This one thought, well impressed upon us, would
suffice to command the utmost awe, reverence, seriousness and devotion whenever we set ourselves to
this matter.

(2) We should also remember who we are who
are to renew vows to be the Lord's. Particularly we
should remember that we are creatures laden with
guilt which we can never expiate, and owing an
obedience that we can never fully pay.

1) We should well remember that we are creatures laden with guilt which we can never expiate,;
and therefore for whom God out of mere pity has
provided a sacrifice which at His table He sets before
us, over the memorials whereof, whenever we come
to receive them, we are to devote ourselves afresh to
the Lord. We should therefore every time, as guilty,
condemned criminals, promise obedience for the
future with the deepest sense of our unworthiness of
that mercy; that must be our only plea for ourselves,
through the merits of another.

2) We should also remember that we are creatures who owe an obedience that we can never fully

pay. Though we vow and vow never so often, we cannot pay the least part of what we vow unless as acted upon and influenced by Him to whom our vows are made. And when we have done our best towards paying our vows and answering our innumerable obligations, there will be much wanting; when we have done all we can, we are but unprofitable servants. God is not in reality a whit the better for all the service we can do Him. The thought of this, well impressed, will keep us from pretending to anything in our own strength; it will lead us to a constant dependance on superior aids; it will prompt us, whenever we renew our vows, to fly to the Holy Spirit, for assistance and help to answer and keep them; and it will prevent our boasting, if at any time by His influence we have been kept in any measure sincere and faithful. Both these considerations taken from ourselves will tend to make us deeply humble out of a sense of our vileness, weakness, and helplessness, whenever we go to give up ourselves to God afresh.

(3) We should also remember for what ends and purposes we vow anew every time we come to the Lord's Table to be the Lord's. In short, there are these two: the more firmly to secure to ourselves His favor, and the more effectually to bind and quicken ourselves to our duty. These are the ends we ought to have in our eye in this matter; and the serious consideration of them will help to make us in earnest, at the time of renewing our vows, and cause us often to think of them afterwards.

DIRECTION 5. *Of the whole sacramental solemnity, select that as the most proper instant for you to give yourself up to Christ, when you are receiving Him and all His benefits into your hands, as I may say, and into your heart.* It may, without all question, be done acceptably enough at other instances during the administration of this ordinance. But the reception of the elements seems to be the most advantageous season. At every sacrament, therefore, when you take the bread and wine as sensible representations of Christ and His benefits, as visible pledges of the love of God through Christ to your soul, give up yourself afresh to God through Christ to live continually in His love and fear, and in strict obedience to His laws till you shall be taken to glory. When the minister, as Christ's messenger, puts the consecrated elements into your hands, then after a thankful adoration of the divine clemency and bounty, expressing itself by such inexpressible gifts as are thereby represented—then, I say, from the bottom of your heart, cry out, "I willingly accept of Thine offered covenant, O Lord. My soul gladly takes Thee for my God and Father, for my Savior and my Sanctifier. And here I give up myself to Thee as Thy own, Thy subject, and Thy child, to be sanctified and saved by Thee, to be beloved by Thee, and to be happy in loving Thee to all eternity. Oh, seal up this covenant by Thy Spirit, which Thou sealest to me in Thy sacrament, that without reserve I may be entirely and forever Thine."

DIRECTION 6. *Every time you, at the sacrament, renew your vows to be the Lord's, take care particularly to vow the death of that corruption that sticks closest to you whereby God is most dishonored, and your comfort and welfare most endangered.* Give it up freely to be sacrificed for Him who gave Himself as a sacrifice for you. Your darling corruption is your nearest, your closest, and one of your most dangerous enemies. Vow therefore to maintain a constant combat against it, that though you can have little hope of completely eradicating it, yet, divine grace assisting you, you will not yield and give way to it; you will not be overpowered by it. Take care expressly to vow an opposition to that which, by its prevalence, would make all your vows ineffectual.

DIRECTION 7. *You should, at every sacrament, not only vow to be the Lord's in general, but to be His in all conditions.* Give up yourself time after time to be disposed of by Him, in all respects, as He shall see good. Take this particularly into your vows at the Lord's Table, that you acquiesce in all the disposals of providence, and are contented in every state whereunto God sees fit to bring you. Disclaim being the carver of your own lot. By your renewed vows willingly resign all that belongs to you to divine management and conduct, and resolve that you will cleave to God whatever it costs you; that though He slays you, yet you will trust in Him; that you will follow Him when He frowns as well as when He smiles; that you will bear His rebukes as the chastisement of a father designed for your good; that you will look on everything as best, whatever He allots you. In a word, resolve that you will entirely resolve your will into His. Doing this at every sacrament seriously would prevent us a great deal of trouble; it would be a spring of peace and comfort to us, whatever our condition, whatever should befall us.

DIRECTION 8. *Take care that the deepest thankfulness is a constant concomitant of all your renewed vows.* There is no greater occasion for thankfulness than this: that we have any ground at all for hope of being accepted upon devoting ourselves to God through Christ; that though past vows have been broken, we may be again accepted upon renewing them; that we have hearts and inclinations to renew them; that we have any ground to hope for strength from heaven to enable us to keep them when we have renewed them; that we have so advantageous a season for renewing them as the sacrament brings with it. All these things minister cause of thankfulness.

Let us, therefore, with a holy exultation of soul, and with that cheerfulness and joy that are the natural indications of a thankful heart, give up ourselves to God from time to time, that it may appear we do not look upon it as a piece of slavery or drudgery, but as our greatest happiness.

These few directions well followed would make sacraments other things than they ordinarily are, and would help us to a much more sensible increase of grace and strength by them than we are wont to receive.

It Is Every Christian's Indispensable Duty to Partake of the Lord's Supper

"This do in remembrance of Me." 1 Corinthians 11:24

by Thomas Wadsworth

These words are a command of the Lord Jesus, received, through revelation, by the apostle Paul, and by him as Christ's herald proclaimed to the church, that not only this particular church of Corinth, but that the whole catholic Church of Christ, in their successive generations until His second coming, might take notice thereof and yield obedience thereto, as to a command of that nature wherein very much of the glory of their once-crucified Redeemer, and their own spiritual joy and consolation, is concerned. This will further appear in the following explication of the words.

In the words you have four parts, two of which are expressed and the other two implied.

I. A duty: "this do."

II. The end for which: "in remembrance of Me."

III. The obligation to the duty: Christ's command. This is implied.

IV. The persons under the obligation: the whole church catholic militant, as far as they are scripturally capacitated thereto. This likewise is implied.

But of these in their order.

I. The duty: "this do." What is this to be done? The Apostle tells you in the beginning of this verse, and in the following verse, and it is this: "This broken bread take and eat; this cup take and drink."

Here is a duty, my brethren, so plain, so easy, of whose obscurity or difficulty certainly we have no cause to complain. For what can be less obscure than a command so evidently expressed, and what can be easier than to eat and drink and call to mind the greatest and best of friends "that loved us and washed us from our sins in His own blood" (Revelation 1:5)? Surely, then, a neglect herein must prove a sin that will admit of no excuse.

But if any of you are offended at the outward meanness of the ordinance, and are thereby tempted to neglect the observance, I wish you to remember who they were that stumbled at Christ Himself because of the poverty of His parents. They say, "Is not this the carpenter's son?" (Matthew 13:55). This was the introduction to their rejecting Christ, and to that great plague that followed, namely, their being rejected by Christ. Certainly, as the meanness of His parents ought not to have prejudiced the glory of His person to those infidels, so ought not the seeming poverty of these elements of bread and wine any way to lessen the glory of that mystery of our redemption that is shadowed out by them. I know, our carnal reasonings are apt to suggest that, since Christ intended to leave behind Him a monument of the greatness of His person in redeeming a church to Himself by His blood, it would have been more suitable to the honor of such an undertaking if the monument had been more magnificent—such as if He had given charge to His disciples to have erected His statue of beaten gold and set it up in the places of their solemn assemblies, like the Roman senate used to do for the honor of their excellent men whose statues they erected in their capitols, or as the London senate does in honor of their kings; they give them their statues in the Royal Exchange.

To this I say that certainly Christ is wiser than man, and that this memorial of Himself, which is already appointed by Him, is more suitable to the end intended than what our vain thoughts have proposed or can propose. For to what end should He have caused such golden statues to have been erected to His memory when He was so acquainted with the nature of man, and with his propensities to idolatry, and, therefore, could not but foresee that at least they would probably make no better use of them than the Israelites did of the brazen serpent, to whom they most unworthily paid that honor that was only due to God Himself? And to show that this is no vain conjecture, I only desire you to call to mind that, though the wisdom of our Savior pitched upon bread and wine, which of all things seem most unfit to make idols of, yet what bad use men have made thereof, and how foolishly their vain minds have transubstantiated them into God, I need not explain to those who know there are Papists in the world, and have heard of their idolatrous doctrine of transubstantiation.

OBJECTION. But, perhaps, some may further urge that, since it pleased our Savior to choose to appoint a feast for His remembrance, it would have been appropriate that His feast should have been more magnificent and, consequently, more significant of the majesty and riches of that Lord whose table it is; but to have only a piece of broken bread and a cup of wine, what poor man could have a meaner entertainment?

This also is easily answered. I say, therefore, that such a pompous feast as you talk of would have not so well comported with His principal end in the institution; for Christ did not in this supper intend the filling of your bellies, but the refreshing of your souls. It was not instituted for the same end as the feast of first-fruits among the Jews, for the remembrance of God's blessing of the earth and giving them full harvests, but for the remembrance of things of a higher nature, of things invisible, spiritual, and eternal: saving you from sin, the law, from the grave and hell —which were all procured by the breaking of Christ's body and the pouring out of His blood for you. Now, your magnificent feasts were not so fit for such a commemoration, for they rather would have tended to have clogged your spirits, making them dull and stupid, and far less apt to have contemplated such divine and heavenly things as those now named are. And, therefore, that this supper is as mean as it is, it is far better than if it were so great and royal as you conceive.

There are others who are well enough satisfied with the wisdom of their Lord, and in the nature of the things appointed for His remembrance, who yet may be, and ought to be, inquisitive as to the reason of them, which I shall reduce to these four questions:

1. Why did the Lord appoint bread rather than any other kind of food?

2. Why must it be bread broken?

3. Why must it be taken and eaten?

4. Why wine as well as bread? And why wine rather than any other drink?

1. To the first I say, He appointed bread as most apt to signify the thing thereby to be presented to our faith; and that is Himself as He is the Bread of life to our souls, for so He calls Himself. John 6:33: "The bread of God is He which cometh down from heaven and giveth life unto the world." And verse 35: "Jesus said, 'I am the bread of life; he that cometh to Me shall never hunger'." This is evident, that man's natural life does not more depend on the virtue of the bread that perishes than the soul's life of grace and glory depends on that virtue that proceeds from a suffering Jesus. The apostle Paul said, "I live, yet not I, but Christ liveth in me" (Galatians 2:20). All that life of faith, all the indwellings of grace in our hearts, come from, and are maintained by, the virtues and influences of Jesus Christ, this "Bread of life." And so, likewise, does our eternal life depend on Him, as He likewise tells us in John 6:27: "Labor for that meat which endureth unto everlasting life, which the Son of Man shall give unto you." This meat is the Lord Himself who, by His sufferings, made our peace and purchased the life of grace and glory for us.

And, indeed, no other meat could so aptly set forth this mystery as bread, because no food is so suitable to a man's nature, none so consistently pleasant, none so strengthening. A man can better subsist with bread without other meats than with any other meats without bread. Thereby, the mystery of conveying soul life to the sinner is excellently set forth; for, as there is other meat for the body beside bread, so there is another way of giving life to the soul beside that of a Savior, and that is an exact obedience to the law of God. But, alas! The sinner, through the weakness of the flesh, can never digest that strong meat, and so cannot live by it. But for a poor, weak, infirmed sinner to be maintained in a life of grace and acceptance with an offended God in and by a Savior is a way of living so suitable to a sinner that men and angels could never have thought of one so suitable; and, therefore, nothing like bread was so fit to set forth this mystery.

2. But why must it be broken bread? Christ Himself acquaints us with the mystical reason thereof in the verse of the text; it is to set forth the breaking of the body of Christ. The breaking of His body must be taken to comprehend all the sufferings of His human nature as united with the divine, as all His soul sufferings (of which there are three phrases used by the evangelists very emphatically, which all signify those dolors of mind He underwent through the dereliction of God), and likewise all the other sufferings of His body, which are set forth by Isaiah with great variety of phrase. Speaking of Christ, he says, "He was despised and rejected of men; a man of sorrows and acquainted with grief" (Isaiah 53:3). And "He hath borne our griefs and carried our sorrows" (verse 4). And "He was wounded for our transgressions; He was bruised for our iniquities; the chastisements of our peace was upon Him, and with His stripes we are healed" (verse 5). And "He was oppressed and He was afflicted" (verse 7). Now all these sufferings were consummated in His crucifixion, "Who His own self bore our sins in His body on the tree" (1 Peter 2:24). These are those sufferings that made that "one sacrifice of Himself" by which He "put away sin" and "hath perfected forever them that are sanctified" (Hebrews 9:26, 10:14). Upon this account it is that the bread of this supper must be

broken before it is taken and eaten. The broken bread is the sign, and Christ's suffering is the mystery signified by it, as I have shown.

3. Why must this broken bread be taken and eaten? This is not without its mystery. Thereby is meant that this breaking, bruising, and wounding of Christ's soul and body were not for any sin of His own, for He was "a lamb without spot" (1 Peter 1:19); but it was for our sins and for our benefit. Our dear Jesus sows in tears and we reap the harvest of His tears in joy. He, by the meritorious extraction of His bloody sweat and agony in the garden, by His tremendous dolors of soul and body on the cross, prepares a medicine, and perfects it by His death; which prepared medicine we, by faith, drink up and, from a state of sin and death, revive. He offered Himself as a good wheat, to be ground by the law and justice of God that, thereby, He might be made "Bread of life" for us by faith to feed on that we may live forever. Therefore, Christ's breaking and giving the bread in this sacrament to His church mystically declares that the sole intention of all His sufferings was for us; and, therefore, He says, "This is the bread that was broken for you." And likewise, taking and eating it further signifies that we profess to believe in Him for life, and wholly rely on Him for acceptance with God, and for the salvation of our souls.

4. But why did He add wine also to this supper and command us to drink thereof in remembrance of Him?

I answer, this addition was for a very good reason, for thereby a further mystery of our salvation by His bloody death is explained.

(1) First, consider that man's natural life is not

maintained by eating only unless he drinks also; for we may die as well by thirst as by hunger. Christ, therefore, by giving us His blood to drink, which is signified by the cup, as well as His body to eat, thereby declares that His suffering death for us is in every way complete and sufficient for the spiritual and eternal life of our souls. So that, as he who has bread and drink lacks nothing to sustain his natural life, so he who has, by faith, an interest in a broken, bleeding Christ lacks nothing to uphold the soul in a state of acceptance with God, or in a condition of spiritual life that is the forerunner and earnest of a life of glory.

(2) But again, if you consider the nature of the drink which He has appointed, it is wine and not water. By it may be signified this much: that as there is no sort of drink so tasteful to the palate, so reviving and strengthening to the spirits, so that spiritual life to which the soul is raised by the death of Christ is a life of the greatest pleasure and joy that is conceivable. For as no liquor like wine cheers a sad, drooping spirit, so nothing so gladdens and cheers the soul as faith in a crucified Christ. Peter said as much in 1 Peter 1:8: "Whom having not seen, ye love, in whom, though now ye see Him not, yet believing, ye rejoice with joy unspeakable and full of glory."

Thus much for the duty: "this do."

II. The end of the duty, and that is: "in remembrance of Me." Here are two things to be inquired into:

1. What reason was there for instituting an ordinance for His remembrance?

2. Why, of all the acts and expressions of His love to

sinners, above all, would He be remembered in His sufferings for us, which is the special signification of this supper?

1. To the first I say, you must call to mind that the time of instituting this supper was the night before that day on which He died. Now the consequence of His death was to be this: that He should be taken from earth to heaven, there to be personally present till the day of judgment. Now, that His church on earth might not forget Him in this long absence, He therefore appointed this supper for the frequent quickening of their remembrance of Him till He comes again.

2. To the other question I answer that the reasons why Jesus would have this act of His love be especially remembered above all others may be these:

(1) Because His dying for the church was the greatest act of love He ever showed His church. Christ said, "Greater love hath no man than this, that a man lay down his life for his friends" (John 15:13). And again, the apostle said, "Hereby perceive we the love of God, because He laid down His life for us" (1 John 3:16). If a man should part with his liberty and suffer bonds, or lay down his estate and become poor, or leave his country and become an exile, for his friend, these would all be expressions of great love; but none of them are comparable to laying down one's life and shedding one's blood for a friend. This last is that wherein Christ has eminently demonstrated His love to His church; this He glories in, and this is that which He would never have His church forget, but frequently remember, in this supper.

(2) Because though He gave, and still does give, very great testimonies of His love to us, such as in His

resurrection, ascension, intercession, preparing glory and, lastly, in His coming again to raise us, justify us, and to take us to Himself to behold and enjoy that glory that He had with the Father before the world was—yet this ordinance is rather for the remembrance of His bloody death for us than for the remembrance of any of the other blessings. And why? Because all these others depend on this. Christ could never have risen for our justification had He not died for the satisfaction of the law and His Father's justice; nor would He have been admitted as an Intercessor, nor have been allowed one mansion in glory for any of us, nor would His Father have suffered Him to have returned again to take any one of us to Himself if He had not, by His death, made our peace, opened the new way into the holy of holies, and purchased a glorious resurrection and an ascension to the heavenly and eternal glory for us. So that, since all His other acts of love toward His church depend on His dying, no wonder if He appointed this supper for the remembrance of His death rather than anything else He either did or promised to do for us.

The conclusion is that, since the end of this ordinance is so glorious, namely the remembrance of the greatest love that ever God the Father or Son showed to us, it cannot but cast a luster and glory upon the duty of coming to this supper, and engage us to a cheerful participation therein.

III. The obligation to this duty, and that is Christ's command. This is implied in the text, but expressed in the foregoing verse. What does the apostle Paul say? "I have received of the Lord that which also I declare unto you." The apostle but declares; the command is Christ's. He is the author of it. It is Christ, not Paul, who said, "This do in remembrance of Me." Christ's commands are the bonds by which we are tied up to obedience; if we break His bonds, we are transgressors. Remember who they were that conspired together saying, "Let us break their bands asunder, and cast their cords away from us." They were those whom the Lord has "in derision" and to whom He will one day "speak in His wrath and vex them in His sore displeasure" (Psalm 2:2–5).

The commands of superiors set out all duty to inferiors, and punish for neglect; and the higher or greater the superior is, the more authority the command has, and the greater punishment will be inflicted on the disobedient. If disobedience to the word spoken by angels received a just recompense of reward, of how much sorer punishment shall they be thought worthy who disobey the command of Jesus Christ (Hebrews 2:2, 10:29)? If a child's disobedience deserves the rod, or a servant's the cudgel, or a subject's the axe or halter, what does disobedience to the Lord Jesus deserve, who is greater than father or master or any earthly sovereign whatsoever? Take heed, then, my brethren, of being found guilty of neglect of this duty that is bound upon you by the command of so great an authority as that of the Lord Jesus who has said, "This do in remembrance of Me."

IV. In the next place are to be considered the persons obliged, and those are the Church of Christ, as far as by scriptural qualifications they are capacitated to a participation therein, who are:

1. Those who can discern the Lord's body in this supper. The lack of this the Apostle gives as the reason of unworthily receiving it, and tells us that they eat damnation to themselves (1 Corinthians 11:29). Now, there are two ways wherein the Lord's body may be said to be discerned in this supper:

(1) When the understanding is spiritually enlightened to perceive the true nature and ends of this supper. And thereby the understanding is enabled to see a greater difference between this and our ordinary meals; for he who shall, for lack of knowledge therein, come to this table with no better preparation, or to no other intents, than when he goes to his own table, certainly perverts the ends of the institution and profanes the ordinance; and therefore he cannot help but incur the great displeasure of God for so doing.

(2) But there is another way of discerning the Lord's body in this supper, and that is by a spiritual taste and relish. For the palate does not have a greater ability of discerning the different relish in the variety of meats man feeds on than the soul of man that has its spiritual senses exercised has in tasting the things of God and judging the different sweetnesses thereof. This is the spiritual faculty that Jesus Christ speaks of when He tells Peter that he savored not the things that are of God, but those that are of men (Matthew 16:23). Now, this you must well observe, you who partake of this supper, whether you relish the love of the Lord Jesus in His dying for sinners, and for you in particular. Is this great love of Christ sweet to your souls, sweeter than honey or the honeycomb? Can you admire the heights and depths of this love, and wonder that the Son of God should take a body to be bruised,

wounded, and slain for the vilest of sinners, among whom you reckon yourself as one? Do you find this love of His for you drawing your hearts to a love of Him, a delight in Him, and a readiness to part with all for Him? This is, indeed, to discern the Lord's body in this supper; and, by this, you are enabled to see a vast difference between this supper and all the feasts of fat things that ever you were at in all your lives. If it is so with you, then you are qualified for this supper, and are, by Christ's command, obliged to partake thereof.

2. Those who have fellowship with God in Christ are those whom Christ has obliged, by His command, to partake of this supper.

This is another qualification which the Apostle gives us in 1 Corinthians 10:18–21 where, discoursing of the nature of divine and likewise of diabolical sacrifices, and of the reason for the priests' and people's eating some part thereof, he also shows the reason for our partaking of the Lord's Table which, though it is not properly a sacrifice that is there offered, yet holds some resemblance to the sacrifices of the law and to the people's eating thereof, inasmuch as it is a commemoration of that one sacrifice which Christ offered up to the Father for our sins; of the benefits of which one sacrifice those who commune at the Lord's Table as effectually partake as if Christ was offered up as often as you there eat and drink.

"Now," says the Apostle, of the legal sacrifices, "they which eat thereof are partakers of the altar" (verse 18); that is, they are partakers of the blessings of that God to whom that altar is erected, and to whom those sacrifices are offered. And not only so, but there is yet a further meaning, which is that those that eat of the altar thereby declare that they take the God of that altar to be their God, from whom they expect all that good they are capable of in this life and that which is to come; and, likewise, they thereby declare that Him, and Him only, will they worship and serve. Now, this engagement of themselves to God, signified by eating of the sacrifice, is that "fellowship" spoken of in verse 20, where the Apostle further tells you that there is the very same intention in those sacrifices that are offered to devils, and the people's eating the feasts that attended those sacrifices. They thereby signified that they took those devils to be their gods and resolved, for the future, to worship and serve them as gods. This is the proper meaning of verse 20: "But I say, that the things which the Gentiles sacrifice, they sacrifice to devils, and not to God: and I would not that ye should have fellowship with devils"; that is, "I would that you would not associate with devils, or enter into a confederacy with them, to serve and worship them, as the idol feasts signify." Now, if the idol feasts signified the confederacy between the devils and their worshippers, so also did the feast that attended the Jewish sacrifice signify a fellowship between the true God and His worshippers, whereby the true God was acknowledged as their God, and that they would worship and serve Him only.

Thus, the Apostle, having illustrated the meaning of eating the Jewish and the Gentile sacrifice, proceeds to accommodate those notions to that of the Lord's table in verse 21: "Ye cannot drink the cup of the Lord, and the cup of devils; ye cannot be partakers of the Lord's table, and of the table of devils." The meaning is this: You cannot serve two such contrary masters as the God and Father of our Lord Jesus, and devils also; for, if you eat of the idols' feasts, you thereby declare that you own devils as gods; and then, coming to the Lord's Table, you thereby declare that you acknowledge only the true God to be your God in and through Jesus Christ, your Sacrifice and Mediator, which practices are very absurd and contradictory.

The conclusion is this: those who partake of the Lord's Table are such who from the heart take the God of that Christ whose death is remembered in that supper to be their God, and who believe that God is really reconciled to them by that sacrifice; and they declare, likewise, hereby that they will worship and serve this God in this Christ, and Him only. Now, if any of you are thus engaged to God in this spirit, you have fellowship with Him, and you are those who have the right to partake of this supper.

DOCTRINE. It is the indispensable duty of all such members of Jesus Christ who can discern the Lord's body in this Lord's Supper, and have fellowship with the Father by this crucified Jesus, to come to this supper and to partake thereof.

There is no point of doctrine that I shall insist on except this one, which is to prove it is your duty to partake of it, and that it is, therefore, indispensable, because the neglect of it is a very great sin.

This I prove by this one argument: Jesus Christ, who instituted it, has commanded you to remember Him in it; and, therefore, if you do it not, you break His command. And what is that but to sin against Him? For what else is a sin but either to do what your God and Savior forbids, or not to do what He commands? This is so plain that it would be a waste of time to use more words to clarify it further. What I have therefore more to say is to show you those many things that accompany this sin, and that tend to aggravate it; so that, when you understand not only that the neglect of this duty is a sin, but that it is a very great one, you may be deterred from continuing in it any longer.

1. I beseech you, consider whose command it is you break. It is the command of the Lord Jesus. To remember Him in this supper is a debt you owe to Him, your Savior, Lord, and Head. It is a command that bears the superscription of the most supreme Authority in heaven or earth; and if, by the sentence of Christ, it was but just to pay the tribute money to Caesar because it bore his superscription, it is much more just for you to pay the tribute of obedience to this command that bears the superscription of an Authority greater than all the Caesars who ever were. What is the name of Caesar in comparison to the name and title of the Son of God, which is a title that speaks Him greater than all angels or archangels in heaven? "For unto which of the angels said He at any time, 'Thou art My Son, this day have I begotten Thee?' " (Hebrews 1:5). This is He whom the prophet Isaiah calls "Wonderful Counselor, the Mighty God, the Prince of Peace"; on whose shoulders it has pleased the "Everlasting Father" to lay the government (Isaiah 9:6). This is He whose kingdom is an everlasting kingdom, and of whose dominion there will be no end (Daniel 4:3); of whom David speaks, "Thy throne, O God, is for ever and ever; a sceptre of righteousness is the sceptre of Thy kingdom" (Psalm 45:6). All power, my brethren, God has given into His hands, and has given Him to bear this royal title, "KING OF KINGS AND LORD OF LORDS"

(Revelation 19:16), and it is He only who is Head of His church. It is this great Lord who has said, "This do in remembrance of Me."

How, then, dare you disobey Him? Believe it, if He has so great authority to command, He has as great a power to punish if He finds you presumptuously disobedient. He who could strike some sick and others dead for profaning this supper can do as much to you for not observing it; and that He does not is not because He lacks power, but because He is gracious, long-suffering, not willing that you should perish for your neglect, but that you may be drawn to repentance, and so to obedience. But, if you are obstinate after you are told thoroughly of your fault, take heed; it will be a horrible thing for you to fall into the hands of a consuming fire.

2. Consider that your neglect of this ordinance is a sin against the command not only of the greatest, but of the best Prince in heaven and earth. He is not only *maximus*, but *optimus* also. This is a further aggravation of your sin. Who ever thought but that Absalom's taking up arms against David was treason? But he who shall consider that the rebellion was against David the man after God's own heart, against David the holiest of men and most just of princes, and, besides all this, against David his father, cannot but judge it an act of the highest treason imaginable. My brethren, in your disobeying this command, you sin against Jesus the Just and Jesus the Gracious; against Him who is by place your Head, in love your Father, in openness of heart your Friend; against Him who emptied Himself that He might fill you, who became poor that He might enrich you, who became an exile from His throne and

Father's kingdom that He might bring you home to your Father's house, who became a curse that you might be blessed, who hung on a tree for you that you might sit on thrones with Him, who called you and washed you from your sins in His blood; and, after all this, when He shall leave such a command as to remember Him in this supper for all His love, how inexcusable must your neglect be, let your conscience be judge with which I leave it.

3. Consider what relation you who are believers stand in to this Jesus who left this command with you. You are the elect of the Father who committed you to His Son to redeem and effectually call you, that He might save you from sin, wrath, the grave, and hell, and bring you to everlasting glory. Why are you called "believers" but from that faith whereby you acknowledge this Jesus as your Lord and your God, whereby you trust in Him and in what He has done and suffered for you, making your peace, procuring your pardon, and opening a new and living way into your Father's kingdom and glory? It is by this faith that you love Him, cleave to Him, and are, therefore, called His friends, His children, His brethren, His subjects, servants, followers, and witnesses. And shall such as you be found disobedient to Him? Shall you carelessly forget to remember Him in a supper appointed by Himself for the remembrance of the greatest act of His love, that is, dying for you?

I tell you, Christ will take it worse from you than from any others. How heinously did David take a contempt from his friend! "Yea, mine own familiar friend, in whom I trusted, which did eat of my bread, hath lifted up his heel against me" (Psalm 41:9). You are

those whom He has chosen out of the world, brought
into His Father's family; and for you to turn the heel
upon Him and refuse to eat at His table is a contempt
that cannot but grieve and anger Him. When Christ
had been teaching that they who did not eat His flesh
and drink His blood had no life in them, at this multitudes were offended and forsook Him; but He said to
His disciples, "Will ye also go away?" implying that, if
they should forsake Him, it would be a matter of
greater trouble than that of the multitudes leaving
Him (John 6:53–67). That the ignorant, profane world
does not come nigh His table does not come so nigh
His heart, but that you believers should withdraw is
that which He must take ill from you. Oh, do not, as
you tender the good pleasure of your Lord, grieve Him
by absenting yourselves from His table.

4. If you consider the command itself, as it is easy,
pleasant, and honorable, your neglect must receive
further aggravation. What is easier than to eat and
drink, or more pleasant to come to a feast, or more
honorable than to feast with the King of kings? Christ
puts you not upon the painful duty of circumcising
your flesh; nor on the troublesome duty of washing
yourselves every time you touch a dead carcass, or what
is ceremonially unclean; nor on the costly duties of
sacrificing your lambs, goats, or oxen; nor on the costly
and toilsome duties of travelling scores of miles every
year to feast before the Lord at Jerusalem, to which the
church of the Jews was bound. He has eased you of all
these burdens and made your task far easier. Instead of
all these, He has instituted but two duties like them:
the one of baptism, the trouble of which you are to
undergo but once in all your lives, and the other of

this supper, which you may have without travelling far for, and which costs you next to nothing.

But, further, it is a duty not less pleasant than easy. What is more pleasant than a feast? And this, of all feasts, is the sweetest; if the perishing manna in the wilderness was so delicious that the taste of it was like wafers made with honey (Exodus 16:31), how much more delicious must this celestial manna, this bread of eternal life, be which is spread before you in this supper! It is a feast of love, of the love of the Father and of the Son; there is a voice in every morsel of bread you there eat, and in every draft of wine you there drink, saying, "Behold, O sinners, how you are beloved of the Father and Son! Had not the Father loved you, He would never have parted with His life for you. Oh, therefore, come to this supper; come, eat, and drink, you beloved of the Lord, and remember His love more than wine. Let all the redeemed of the Lord come hither and praise Him."

Nor is it a duty less honorable than pleasant. It is a pleasant thing to feast, but it is honorable to feast with a king, most honorable with the King of kings and Lord of the whole earth. How did Haman glory that he was invited to the banquet with the king! He reckoned it not as his task, but his privilege; not as his work, but as his reward. And shall a feast with an earthly, mortal king be more valued than a feast with the heavenly and immortal God? This supper is the Lord's supper; it is the great God who has made the provision, and it is His eternal Son who has made the invitation. Oh, take heed of excuses; for, though you make them, God will not take them! Make, therefore, yourselves ready; put on your wedding garments and come away. Do not let a table so well furnished lack its guests lest Christ lose the honor and you lose the comfort of the entertainment. But, if you will still draw back, know not only that you sin, but that your sin is great because it is a command that is so easy, sweet, and honorable, as I have shown you this is.

5. There is one circumstance more in the command which should quicken you to the observance, and that is the time when this command was given. It was the very night in which He was betrayed, the very last night He lived on the earth, the night before that day in which He offered up Himself as a sacrifice to justice for us. Then it was that He said, "Do this in remembrance of Me." What is this but as if He had said, "My friends, I am now to leave you and be taken out of your sight; but oh, let Me not be out of your mind! Tomorrow, you shall see how I love you when you see Me scorned of men, deserted by God, praying, groaning, bleeding, dying for you. Oh, let not that love of Mine be forgotten! And, lest it should, I therefore institute this supper, charging you with My whole Church that, till I come again, as often as they eat this bread and drink this cup, they remember Me."

This is the charge of our dying Lord; and, surely, if we have any love for Him, we should not dare but observe it. When Jacob was dying, he gave the charge, as some of his last words, that Joseph should forgive the unkindness of his brethren; and, when he was dead, the brethren thought it a good argument to move Joseph to take pity on them. They, therefore, "sent a messenger unto Joseph saying, 'Thy father did command before he died saying, "Forgive, I pray thee now, the trespass of thy brethren." ' " This argument broke

Joseph's heart. It is said that "he wept when they spake unto him, and said, 'Fear not' " (Genesis 50:16–19). Oh, how did the words of his dying father move and melt him! I think I can hear him saying, "Was this the desire of my dying father? I cannot then but yield. Would my father have me forgive? I freely do it."

Now, my brethren, why should you not do as much for your dying Jesus as Joseph did for his dying Jacob? Was Jacob his father? Jesus is our Savior. Did Jacob love Joseph? But he did not die for him as Jesus did for us; and shall we find a heart to deny our Lord in His dying request when Joseph could not find one to deny his father? Oh, then, as Joseph forgave, so let us do this in remembrance of Him, which will be an instance of that great love and honor we keep for His memory!

6. In the next place, I desire you to think of the contempt you throw upon this ordinance by your neglect. What is it but that you have slight thoughts of the authority of the Institutor, and very mean thoughts of the institution itself? And is not this to proclaim to the world that there is, in your judgment, a command of the Lord Christ, and a duty in the Christian religion, that is frivolous and childish, not worth observing? Believe it, the world will judge it by your practice, and not by your profession.

The Rechabites would drink no wine because Jonadab, the son of Rechab, forbade them; nor will the Turks drink wine because that impostor Mohammed forbade them. Thus the one honored their father, and the other honored their false prophet; and will you who are Christians let these men rise up in judgment against you? Shall error be more prevalent with them than truth is with you? And will you let the Turks outdo you in honoring a false prophet more than you do the true? Is Mohammed dearer, and are his institutions more sacred to his followers, than Jesus Christ and His institutions are to you? Christ bids you to drink of this cup in remembrance of Him, and you will not; but Mohammed forbids them wine and they obey him. You judge now; who gives the greatest honor—they to Mohammed or you to Christ? I think you should blush to think of it. O Christians, for shame amend and give no more occasion to Christ's ministers to reprove you for so gross a sin.

7. I have not yet done. Think once more with what hypocrisy this neglect is accompanied. What is hypocrisy but to endeavor to seem better than indeed we are—to seem zealous for Christ and His ordinances when, in truth, we are lukewarm and indifferent? You are Protestants by profession; your fathers were so before you, and you seem ready to plead their cause. Oh, that you would look back and consider the age past! With what zeal was this ordinance pleaded for in King Henry VIII's and Queen Mary's day! The papists would give you the bread only, but you would have the cup also; they would have you adore the bread as God, but you would not commit so great idolatry; for which cause how many were exiled, how many imprisoned, racked, hanged, or burned! And, after all these heats— oh, gross hypocrisy!—you will have neither bread nor wine, nor will you take it in the gospel way without the encumbrances of superstition and idolatry.

You talk of popery returning, and truly not without ground; for when I consider how we slight this ordinance, rescued from the papists with the expense of so much blood, I think it is but a righteous thing with

God to bring us under their own yoke again; and, if it comes to that, then you would be glad of this ordinance, if you could get it. Then you will be brought into this strait: either you must take it in the popish way and be damned for your idolatry, or in the gospel way and be burned at a stake for opposing Antichrist. Oh, repent in time, renew your first love, strengthen your zeal that is ready to die. Come to the Lord's Table as you are invited; take it in His way, that is, with knowledge, faith, love, and thankfulness, lest you provoke the Lord by your neglect to take it quite away from you, as He is likely to do if He allows popery to return.

8. Consider again how scandalous you are in this neglect. There are not a few about this kingdom who are ancient Christians, who have had for a long time the reputation of wisdom, sobriety, and godliness in their lives, but who yet are notoriously guilty in this matter. I beseech such to consider their scandal herein. What is it, my brethren, to scandalize weak brethren but to lay stumbling blocks in the way of such over which they may fall and, if not ruin themselves, yet at least wound their peace? When weak Christians see such as you live in the neglect of this ordinance, what do they do but, by your example, take encouragement to neglect it also? It is likely that they reason like this: "If there were any necessity of partaking of that supper, why do not such and such do it? They are godly, wise men; surely if they thought it was a sin, they would not persevere in this neglect."

And so are the weak emboldened to sin, though against their light; for it is scarcely possible that they should read or hear of so plain a command as, "This do in remembrance of Me" and not be, in some measure, awakened to the sense of their duty; which light they yet stifle because of your example. I beseech you, therefore, by the mercies of God, the love of the Lord Jesus, and the compassion you ought to have for your weak brethren, that you would not give such a manifest occasion for them to fall and wound their soul, if not for their destruction.

9. Once again, let me entreat you to lay to heart how unworthily hereby you cast contempt upon the practice of the churches of Christ in all ages past. Tell me, if you can, what church of Christians, for sixteen hundred years, has not been conscientious about this duty. In Justin Martyr's time, by what we can gather from his writings, it seems that the church always closed its solemn public meetings with this supper. And Augustine tells us that there were Christians in his day who favored taking it every day of the week. And, though he himself thought such daily participation thereof was not needful, yet he persuaded the people to partake thereof every Lord's Day. Now, though Christ has not expressly tied us to such a frequency, yet He intimated to us that He would have Himself remembered herein very often when He said, "As often as ye eat this bread." But for you to live in a perpetual neglect is very far from taking it often. It was a saying of Asaph, "If I say, 'I will speak thus,' behold, I should offend against the generation of thy children" (Psalm 73:15). Oh, that you would consider that, as long as you continue this neglect, you offend against the children of God in many generations, even from the time of the institution!

10. Lastly, think how unmerciful you are to your

own souls in denying them this ordinance. What do you do but withhold their proper and necessary food from them? You call upon them to exercise their graces, and you find them faint and languid. You then complain of them, "Oh, what a dead and listless heart do I have to God and duty!" Alas, man! It is your own fault! You, like an Egyptian taskmaster, call for the tally of brick and deny straw! You call to your soul to do her work, and will you not give her the bread to refresh her which her Savior has allowed? Bring your soul to this supper, feed her, satisfy her with a crucified Jesus who is here presented, and then tell me whether her faith will not strengthen, her love increase, her joys and consolations multiply. Ask your brethren what tastes and relishes, what sweet refreshments they have received from the Lord in this ordinance. They will cry unto you, "Oh, come, taste and see how gracious God is to us at this feast!"

It was a saying of Bernard: "When my strength fails me, I am not troubled, I do not despond. I know a remedy; I will go to the Table of the Lord. There I will drink and recover my decayed strength." And, I dare say, that good man experienced no more than what ten thousand of the Lord's people frequently experience. Where would you have Christ give you His love but in His garden of spices, in His wine-cellar, where His banner over you is love? Here it is that He broaches His side and lets out His heart's blood to you, which is sweeter to a believing sinner than the most delicious banquet to the most hungry appetite; and, if it does not prove so to all who come, it is because of their own dispositions, and not because of any deficiency in the ordinance itself.

Objections and Answers

And now I would be done, were it not that I understand there are some objections to be removed, which I shall propose and answer, and then leave you to the blessing of the Lord to give you a full satisfaction in the whole matter.

OBJECTION 1. But some may say, "All that you have been hitherto pleading for is but a ceremony; and, surely, God will not be so much concerned with a failure in so small a punctilio as a ceremony!"

ANSWER. True, it is a ceremony; but it is one that bears the stamp of the authority of the Lord Jesus. If He appoints it, will you slight it and say, "It is but a ceremony"? But again, if it is a ceremony, it is the most glorious one that was ever appointed, inasmuch as it is designed to set forth the redemption of the world as it was completed and perfected by the death of Jesus Christ. Yet again, it is but a ceremony; but you are greatly mistaken if you think that, therefore, there is no danger in neglecting it. What was the tree of the knowledge of good and evil but a ceremony? Yet, as for the disobedience in eating thereof, do you not know and feel what wrath it has brought on the whole race of mankind? And, tell me, was circumcision any more than a ceremony? Yet it almost cost Moses his life for neglecting to circumcise his son; for the angel stood ready with his sword to slay him if he had not prevented it by his obedience (Exodus 4:24–25). So for the Lord's Supper, as much a ceremony as it is, yet for the abuse of it, some of the church were sick and weak, others fell asleep, that is, they died (1 Corinthians

11:30). And if God so severely punished the abuse, how do you think to escape who presumptuously neglect the use thereof?

OBJECTION 2. "But if I am regenerate and have become a new creature, I am sure I shall be saved. I do not fear that God will cast me away for the disuse of a ceremony."

ANSWER. Is this the reasoning of one regenerate? Surely you do not understand what regeneration means. Is it not the same as being born of God? And is not he who is born of God a child of God? And what is it to be obedient to the Father but to do as He commands? And has He not commanded you by His Son to remember your Savior in this Supper? When you have considered this, then tell me what you think of this kind of reasoning: "I am a child of God; therefore, I will presume to disobey Him. He bids me remember Jesus in this supper and I will not." I think you blush at the very mention of it; and what if He should cast you quite off for this neglect? Yet you have no reason to think but that either outwardly or inwardly, or both, He will scourge you for this sin before you die; and examine whether the languor of your graces and poverty of your consolations are not the lashes of your heavenly Father for this sin.

OBJECTION 3. "But I see a crucified Savior in the Word read and preached. I see Him there lifted up and dying for me, and I bless God to my great comfort. How needless a thing is it, then, to remember Him in this Supper so!"

ANSWER. Vain man would be wiser than Christ, who is the wisdom of His Father. Jesus Christ has seen fit to command that He should be preached to His church, but also remembered in this supper. But you say (oh, presumption!) that the first was sufficient, and that the latter is needless and impertinent. Will you undertake to give counsel to the Son of God or advise Him in the affairs of His kingdom? Shall the Holy Ghost say, "He was faithful over His own house as a Son" (Hebrews 3:5–6), and will you accuse Him of weakness in His administrations? "He that reproveth the Son of God, let him answer it" (Job 40:2).

But why should you say, "This supper is needless because Christ is remembered in the Word"? May not truth in some cases be more effectually conveyed to the soul by the eye than the ear? Do you not find yourselves more moved to see the execution of a man, to see one hanged or beheaded, than simply to hear the story of it? Jesus Christ in this ordinance is, as it were, crucified before your eyes, in a manner more affecting than when you only hear of His crucifixion by the Word. But further, this supper has further ends than the Word preached; for Christ, and the covenant of grace founded in His blood, is preached to the intent that you may believe and enter into this covenant with God. But the Supper is instituted as an outward sign to ratify this covenant between God and you after it has once been entered into by faith. You do not think it enough in marriage to take one another's word, but you complete it by a solemn vow in the presence of witnesses. I tell you, Christ has not thought it enough to take your word, but He will have it confirmed solemnly by this ordinance, and He will have it often repeated, for He knows us too well as to our proneness to backsliding which, by this supper, He would prevent.

But, yet further, who is it that dares presume to give Christ His measures, how, and where, and by what means He should manifest Himself and His love to His believers? What if He has reserved some peculiar degrees of light and strength and comfort to convey to His people by this Supper that He does not see fit ordinarily to do by His Word? And if it is so, who shall say to Him, "Why are you doing this?" I remember what is recorded of the two disciples travelling to Emmaus. By their discourse, it appeared that they doubted whether Jesus was the Christ. Christ, meeting with them, and perceiving that their faith staggered, took this method: first, He endeavored to settle them in their faith that, notwithstanding He had been crucified and buried, yet He was the true Christ; which He did by expounding Moses and the prophets, from whence He proved that it was necessary that Christ must suffer. And this was with good effect upon their hearts; for they said, "Did not our hearts burn within us while He talked with us by the way?" But, yet, He reserved a fuller manifestation of Himself to them until He came to break bread with them at their house. Then it is said, "Their eyes were opened and they knew Him" (Luke 24:13–32). I do not say that breaking bread in that place was the Lord's Supper in the sense in which I speak of it, but it will serve me so far as to illustrate what I intend, which is this: that it may be the pleasure of Christ to entail peculiar manifestations of Himself to His people upon certain ordinances. He will beget faith by the preaching of the Word, and set your hearts in a flame of love for Him from what you hear there, and yet may reserve the confirmation of your faith, and the establishment of your love for Him, to be wrought by the Lord's

Supper, which is that which many of His people have experienced. And, therefore, it cannot be said to be in vain to have Christ presented to you in the Lord's Supper as well as in the Lord's Word preached. And this I conceive abundantly enough to silence this objection.

OBJECTION 4. "But I am not prepared worthily to receive and, therefore, I dare not come to this table lest I eat and drink damnation to myself."

ANSWER. Whose fault is that? What have you been doing all your life? If you have not been "working out your salvation with fear and trembling," you have done nothing! Repentance has been preached; why has not your heart been broken? Christ has been offered; why have you not received Him by faith? This supper has been explained; why have you not understood it? If you had but repented of your sins and believed in the Lord Jesus and understood the meaning of this supper, you would have been prepared for a worthy receiving of it. But, if it is not thus with you, it is your own fault. Therefore, get into your closet; humble yourself mightily before the Lord for this long abuse of the means of grace, and pray Him to give you that repentance, faith, and knowledge that may make you worthy. And be assured that God is merciful, gives liberally to those who ask, and upbraids no man (James 1:5). "Ask and it shall be given you; seek and ye shall find" (Matthew 7:7). But, if you will not be at these pains, your unworthiness is voluntary and your complaint of unfitness is mere hypocrisy; and then remember the many woes pronounced against hypocrites.

Yet there may be some children of God who are prepared, but yet dare not come because they do not understand that they are prepared.

To these I say, if, through ignorance of your own state, you are kept off, why do you not come to such ministers whom you judge faithful to help you? You will carry your evidences to men skillful in the law to judge of your title to an earthly inheritance; and, if your body is under some distemper, you will ask your physician what he thinks of you. Why, then, will you not go to some able minister and ask his judgment of you and desire his directions? I dare say, this course would set many a weak Christian at liberty from his doubts and perplexities which have and may so entangled him that he has not seen his right to his privileges. So he may go on in this darkness, for all I know, to his death. Be persuaded, therefore, to take advice.

The conclusion is this: I would that all of you whose consciences bear you witness that you are the Lord's people, and that you have given yourselves up to Christ, would take a resolution to be obedient to the Lord in coming to this supper as He has commanded; and, as you have heard this morning, take heed of sinning against light with your eyes wide open upon it. Sins of ignorance God may wink at; but, when you sin presumptuously, though it is against the least command, and persevere in it, I question whether it is consistent with salvation. But if it is, doubtless, it will be a salvation through the fire. May the Lord give you understanding!

Self-Examination

"Commune with your own heart upon your bed."
Psalm 4:4

by Joseph Alleine

DOCTRINE. It is the great duty of every man to be often conferring with and taking an account of his own heart. 2 Corinthians 13:5: "Examine yourselves," prove yourselves; know you not your own selves? It is the duty of a man not to take the report of his heart, but he must search his heart. He must be often putting questions to his heart. The heart cannot be easily found out. The reasons for this point are these two:

REASON 1. The first reason is taken from the difficulty of coming to know our own hearts. Therefore it is a necessary duty, because it is so hard to know our own hearts. Now this appears, first, because men are so generally mistaken in their own hearts, both bad men and good men. How often do bad men boast of their good hearts? And, though our Savior tells us that out of the heart proceed evil thoughts, yet all the while they think their hearts are good. They see nothing of these things in their hearts.

When Hazael heard of his heart, he wondered that he should have such a heart. He would not believe that there was such a cruel nature in his heart. He thought it was for dogs and tigers to do this; and yet, afterwards, he did all this.

And so it is for good men. How Peter failed in this, saying he would die for Christ. And Christ could scarcely put him out of this conceit. And it is likely that he intended what he spoke. Yes, he tried more than the rest did, for he only drew his sword. And who would have thought that there was that swearing and cursing in his heart as there was. So it was with David's adultery (2 Samuel 11).

Second, it appears in that it has cost men so dearly to know their own hearts.

1. It has cost them sharp trials. Deuteronomy 8:2: "God led thee these forty years in the wilderness to know what was in thine heart," that is, to make *you* to know. One would have thought that they had never been guilty of such horrid unbelief to distrust God when they fed upon and witnessed miracles.

2. It has cost them many sad falls to know them. Neither Hezekiah nor anyone else would ever have thought that there could be that in his heart after God wrought a miracle for him; and yet God left him that He might try what was in his heart (2 Chronicles 32:31). Brethren, take heed that you are not too sure of your own hearts; be often fearful of your own hearts.

3. It has cost them many tears and prayers to know them. Though some of God's people have been students of their own hearts twenty or forty years, yet, after all this, they find, sometimes, that their hearts are too hard for them.

Third, the difficulty of this appears because the saints have called in the special help of God, without which they could not come to know it. So David

said in Psalm 139:23, "Search me, O God." Our own
hearts are too hard for us unless we take God's special assistance with us. Our hearts will deal with us
without this assistance as a bad neighbor will do
when we come to search for our goods. They will not
let you in unless you come with the king's officers.

Now the difficulty of this lies:

1. In that the heart of man is so deep.
Ecclesiastes 7:24: "That which is exceedingly deep,
who can find it out?" Now so is the heart of man, for
so it says in Psalm 64:6: "And the heart is deep." The
heart of man is deep as earth; yea, as hell (James
3:6), that is, the hell that is in the heart.

2. The heart is very dark (Ephesians 4:18):
"Having their understanding darkened." There you
have two parts of the misery of man in his natural
estate.

(1) He is a stranger to God.

(2) He is a stranger to himself. He cannot see
a jot into his own heart until the Lord springs into
the soul with a new light as He did into the prison.
He cannot see what is there in his heart. And we do
not need any further evidence for this than that
common good opinion that men have of their
hearts. Though their hearts are full of odious poison and the like, yet they cannot see it until God
opens their eyes by conversion, and then they see it.
But yet it is but candlelight that the best of us have
here to illumine our own hearts.

3. Because the heart is very deceitful above all
things. There have been great deceits in the world;
yet, put all together, none in the world is as cunning
as the heart. There is no comparison. You would

think that, if a man were told beforehand that a known cheater was coming to deal with him, he would take heed of dealing with him. Such a man would surely think that he should not be too hard for him; but yet the saints have known this, that the heart is so deceitful, and they have been twenty or forty years learning it. Yet their hearts are too hard for them.

REASON 2. The knowledge of the heart is so exceedingly necessary. If a man turned over all the books in the world, and is not learned in his own heart, it is nothing.

USE. The use is to stir us up to know our own hearts. I beseech you, whatever you neglect, do not neglect this duty.

Now there are sundry ways of communing with our own hearts. Sometimes, it is by way of consolation. "Return to thy rest, O my soul" (Psalm 116:7). Sometimes it is by way of expostulation. "Why art thou cast down, O my soul?" (Psalm 42:5). Sometimes it is by way of exhortation, to quicken and excite our hearts. Psalm 62:5: "My soul, wait thou only upon God." Here he stirs up his heart in believing in God.

So "wake up my glory," that is, my heart or soul. The soul of man is his honor (Genesis 49:6). And see how David exhorts his soul, "up my heart, my glory." He found his heart, it may be, somewhat dead and dull; and, therefore, he stirs it up, sometimes by way of instruction (Psalm 16:2, 7).

But sometimes he does it by way of examination and inquiry, and that is the principal way on which all the rest depend. Therefore, I intend to insist on that; and I beseech you to stir up yourselves to this duty. My brethren, you should often question your own hearts. It is hard to think how papists, yea, pagans, surpass us in this. And what a shame is it that we should be strangers to this duty—especially after we have been told of it, and have confessed that it is a duty!

Now you must know there is a double communication: ordinary and extraordinary. Ordinary communications are either transient or more solemn. The first type we should be in continually, every hour in the day. The lack of this is the reason that we are such strangers to our own hearts. Christians, remember this and step often into your own heart and thoughts. The heart of man is always talking to itself, and you should often step in and see what it is that the heart and thoughts are talking about. See if they are well employed; and, if they are not, give them a task, especially before, in, and after duties— most especially after duties, to search what evil we have committed in the duty, or else we shall not find matter for examination of our hearts in the evening. We should take notes of our hearts all day, and read them over in the evening.

And then, besides this, there must be a solemn examination. And here I would beseech you Christians, every evening, to spend some time for this work, a quarter or half an hour. I speak of the evening, because the Scripture speaks so much of this time, and the practice of good men has been in this time. A very heathen could do this, and you shall find this was David's practice. Psalm 16:7: "My reins instruct me in the night season." Well, then, I would advise you, Christian, to take this advice.

Every evening, before you sleep, set some time apart, more or less, from the world, and set your heart as in the presence of God. And charge it before God to answer to these interrogations.

First, with reference to your duties:

1. Did not God find me on my bed when He looked for me on my knees? This question might be a shaming question, and I cannot, without indignation, speak of this. Many of us are so willing to please ourselves with a little ease, when we should enjoy those pleasant hours with God! How do you think that God will take this at your hands? There are many persons who spend many hours in their beds so that they might enjoy communion with God, and then they are willing to shuffle up their duties in a corner. I beseech you that this may be left off.

It may be that many of you do not have as much to do in the world as others. You do not have the business that others have and, therefore, you do not need to rise as early, but may lie longer than others. Ah, Christian! Do not make use of the fact that you have more time for sloth than others! I tell you this from God: He has not given you any time to be idle in.

I am afraid that many of you do not know what it is to sleep by rule. If you do not, this is a shame to you. A Christian should do nothing but by rule.

It may be that some will say, "What rule must we use?" I answer, we must have respect to our bodies. What may be for one man may not be for another; but for healthy bodies, six or seven hours is enough in conscience. Let every man give his body no more than his body will require. And remember this general rule: be sure that you use some self-denial about your sleep. That general rule should be observed, though the particular rule cannot be given. That excellent servant of God, Mr. Jordan, who kept assurance of God's love for thirty years, got up at three or four o'clock every morning and, if he did not, he bewailed it. Oh, that it were thus with you!

2. Have I not prayed to no purpose, or let roving thoughts eat out my duty? Take an account every evening what you have gained by that day's prayers. If we did so, this would be splendid, and then we would grow quickly. But it is our great loss that we content ourselves with the duty done, and do not look to the manner of performance. Therefore, if you would gain by your duties, see how as well as what you prayed. How did I pray? Was my heart lively or dull? Do not let it be enough that your hearts acquit you in this, that you have not neglected duty, but whether you have been slack in the duty. And because vain thoughts are our great enemies here, look that these do not eat up your sacrifice. We have often complained of these, but we are not relieved of them. And what is the reason? Because we do not take our hearts to task for our vain thoughts in duty every day. If we did but ask our hearts this every evening, our hearts would be ashamed to be found guilty every day.

3. Have I not neglected, or been very careless in, the reading of God's holy Word? I am afraid that many of us neglect this duty. Does not many a day pass over our heads wherein we do not read even a chapter? And yet I fear more the manner in which

you read. Did you begin with prayer, and observe what promises, what commands, what threatenings or examples were there for you to imitate, or fear, or avoid? And did you turn it into prayer afterwards? I would advise you to do that, to turn some of the chapter into prayer afterwards. Oh, that we should slight the Word that the saints of God have set such a price upon! The Word! Why, 'tis the Word of God, and when we see the hand of God on it, this should affect us!

4. Have I digested the sermon I heard last? Have I prayed it over and repeated it over? Brethren, would you know why we are such dwarfs in Christianity, why we grow so little? Here is one grand reason: we take in much and digest but little. It may be that you are greedy of taking opportunities. There cannot be a sermon but you must be in attendance or else it is not well; but do you pray it over and repeat it over again? The lack of this is the reason why we grow no better. Therefore, do not content yourself that you have heard such a sermon. It is never well until God hears of it in confession, prayer, and praise for such mercies as were revealed to you. This is the way to thrive, and you will never thrive until you come to this. The reason why there has been so much sowing and so little fruit is that the seed has not been covered by meditation and watered by prayer. The devil, or evil thoughts, come and steal away the seed.

5. Was there not more of custom and fashion in my family duties than there was of conscience? Brethren, if my observation does not fail, Christians are more apt to be formal in these duties than in others. Now, this should be a cause of shame to us.

This is a very great evil. We are very formal in such duties as come ordinarily, especially if we are not the speaker, but join with others; whereas, if you made use of it, thankfully to prize and gladly improve such opportunities, you would thrive more abundantly. Say to yourself, "Now I have an opportunity to worship God in the family."

You who are heads of families, it is a great mercy that you have, that you can lead your families into the presence of God; and you who are members of the family have a great mercy beyond many others, that you live in a family where you can come twice a day at least to God. And do you labor to improve it?

6. Where have I denied myself today for God? Brethren, you have not lived like Christians this day if so be that you have not used some self-denial today. If you have not denied your flesh, but have given it as much ease as it would have, if you have let your appetite have as much as it would, if you have let your tongue go out wherever it would, you have not lived as a Christian.

7. Have I redeemed my time from overly long and needless visits, idle imaginations, fruitless discourses, unnecessary sleep, and a pre-occupation with needs of the world? It is a duty incumbent upon every Christian to redeem his time. This has sat heavy on the best of God's servants, that they have not redeemed their time more than they have. Now, if you would redeem your time, these time-robbers and devourers must be watched:

(1) First, overly long and needless visits. Many men are so long in their visits that they lose much of their own time, and the time of others whom they

go to visit. Ask your heart, "Have I not been too long in such a visit, and did I not steal away others' time as well as my own?" And so for needless visits when there is no purpose. Be sparing and short in your visits, or else you will lose your time, and make others to lose their time also.

(2) Second, idle imaginations. These steal away our time, and we do not think about it. If this were looked to, how might we grow in grace? When a man is on his journey, how might he have good thoughts; whereas our hearts are talking of vanity, and so it is in our shops.

(3) Third, fruitless discourses. Ask your heart whether you have not failed in this duty. What a shame is this, that when many Christians come together, there is scarcely anything of God in their mouths while they are together.

(4) Fourth, unnecessary sleep. There is much evil in this, when persons take up so much time in their sleep that there is scarcely any time left for religious duties.

(5) Fifth, pre-occupation with needs of the world. Men must be very watchful of this, or else the world will rob them of their time. If a man will not use some self-denial about his worldly occasions, but serves God no more than the world will give him leave, he shall serve God only a little.

8. Have I done anything more than ordinary for the Church of God in a time extraordinary? Brethren, we shall never be able to stand before our own consciences in the evil day if our hearts cannot acquit us in this, that we have put ourselves to it more than an ordinary amount for the Church of

God. You know the troubles of the Church at this day, and we should, every one of us, run with his bucket and put out this fire. God is crying to us as Moses did to Aaron (Numbers 16:46): "Take a censer and go quickly unto the congregation, and make an atone-ment for them; for there is wrath gone out from the Lord, the plague is begun." Oh, let us run, for the tokens of His displeasure are in the land! It is your tears that must quench these flames that the bush, the Church, is burning in. How is it that we do not weep over the Church? We sit here at ease through God's blessing, but how is it with the Church of God abroad in the land? How far are our hearts from the temper of God's worthies heretofore? It was said of one holy woman that, when there was any bad news concerning the Church, people sought to conceal it from her lest her heart should be overwhelmed with the news of it.

If we had some certain news that our estates were in danger, how would we break out of our sleep! And yet how is it that we are so careless of the Church of God! How is it that others are so wounded and sick, and ready to die with grief, and yet we take so little notice of it? One has said to me, "I wonder how any can laugh when God's Church is in such distress."

I beseech you to take some more time with God than you were wont to heretofore for the Church of God. If you have prayed twice a day heretofore, perhaps you can pray three times a day, adding another quarter of an hour to seek God for the Church, and sometimes even taking the whole day, it will come in upon your account, when the troubles come upon the Church, that you labored with your bucket, if it were possible, to put out the fire.

9. Have I been careful about my company? Many times many of us are very great losers by having vain company. To be sure, if they do us no other harm, they rob us of our time, and that is no small hurt. And, therefore, fly from their company as from a plague-sore. Or if sometimes your calling calls you to them, yet do not go among them before you have prayed to be delivered from the evil of their company.

10. Have I not neglected some relative duty today, as of husband, wife, parent, child, master, or servant?

Thus much for the interrogations regarding duties.

Now, second, for the questions regarding your sins.

1. Does not sin sit light? This is the cause of no small mischief to our souls. This is the cause why Christ is no more precious, and the promises no more sweet, because sin sits so light. Why can we hear the gospel as a common, lovely thing, and be but little affected with it? If you could get a greater sense of sin upon your spirit, this would be a speedy course of preventing sin. This is a cutting down of a great limb of sin. When a man cuts down a limb of the tree, a great deal of brush will come down with it; and so, if you cut down this limb, let sin sit heavy, down come self and pride, and many sins will come down with it. How is it that Paul could say, "O wretched man that I am," and we are no more distressed with the sense of sin?

2. Am I a mourner for the sins of my land? My brethren, we have great reason to check ourselves sharply here, that when God has made it so plainly a duty to us, yet we are so little affected with the sins of the land. When God sets a mark upon them for preservation, who cry for all the abominations that are done in the midst of the land, yet we remain insensible! Can our hearts acquit us now in this thing? Oh, let us never leave our hearts, but be checking them for this.

If your name were wounded, it would almost break your heart; and yet how is it that we can hear of God's name being dishonored and yet not break for it? Can our hearts witness for us that we never hear of the blasphemy that is in the land, and of the superstition and idolatry of the land, but God hears of it again by us, before we sleep, by prayer? This should be a lamentation to us that the wounds that are given to God are no more upon our hearts. We may say of the glory of God as they said of David in 2 Samuel 18:3, "'tis worth ten thousand of us." Our estates, and names, and all that is dear to us, yea, our very souls, are not worth as much as the honor of God. And how is it then that we can see God dishonored and we cannot mourn for it? God's glory is His crown that is upon His head; and shall we see His crown trodden down in the dirt and not be affected with it? We are far from the disposition of God's saints and servants heretofore.

When Moses saw the idolatry of the people, he was so zealous that he overturned the tables that God wrote with His own finger. When the people had taken strange wives, Ezra sat down and rent his clothes (Ezra 9). Brethren, how may we blush to hear and read this, and to think how far our hearts are from this frame!

It may be that you think it enough that you cried out when you heard the blasphemy so that you are free from it yourselves, but this is your sin if you do not mourn over it. No doubt the godly Corinthians detested the sin in 1 Corinthians 5:2–7, but the Apostle told them that this was not enough. They were to mourn over it. When wickedness reigns, it is, as it were, the time of the devil's incarnation. It is as if hell itself were broken loose upon us to act its part above ground, and we are not mourning over it.

3. Do I not live in something that I know or fear to be a sin? If you do this, there is no peace with God or conscience to be had for you. Psalm 66:18: "If I regard iniquity in my heart, God will not hear my prayers." It is a sign that God does not regard you if you are one who lives in the practice or allowance of any sin; and He will not own you for this. If you yield up yourself to any sin willingly, that is a manifest sign that you are none of God's (Romans 6:16).

So much for questions about your sin.

Now, third, for questions regarding your heart. Ask these several questions.

1. Have I been much in holy ejaculations? Thus we ought to pray continually; not only at our set and solemn times, but upon all occasions, to step aside and speak a word or two with God, in our journeys and occupations. This is walking with God indeed, when we do not only take a turn or two with Him in the morning and again in the evening, but all the

day long. It is said of Mr. Dod that he never got upon his horse but he prayed before he got off.

Thus did Nehemiah; while the King was talking with him, he was praying to God. Nehemiah 2:4: "So I prayed to the God of heaven." This was a heavenly ejaculation. This would keep your hearts praying all the day long. When the hearts of men naturally bend to God as the sparks fly upward, this is a good thing indeed—when we cannot go by the door but we must step in and have a turn with God.

You will take it as a great kindness for a man not only to come at set times to visit you, but when he comes in every time he passes by the door to see you. And when your heart is thus wont to turn into God, this will be an evidence to you that your heart is used to conversing with God.

2. Has not God been out of mind, and heaven out of sight? Put that question to your heart. My brethren, this is our great sin, and should be our great shame, that the thoughts of God are such strangers to our souls, that we are so little in heaven during the day as we are. Oh, what a loser is God by this denial of His glory! What losers are we by this in our graces and comforts! Oh, were our hearts, on all occasions, thus thinking of God, how holy a frame should we quickly grow into! Why should not our hearts be as much with God as the hearts of the worldlings are with the creature? Does not God deserve it as much as the creature?

The creature's heart is always talking with the world. If he comes to hear, his heart is talking with the world. If he comes to pray, his heart is always with the world. Why should not our hearts be talk-

ing with God while our hands are employed about
this world? It was a heavenly breathing of a gracious
spirit that produced this challenging passage:

> Lord, as formerly I lived without Thee in the
> world, so now let me live without the world in
> Thee. If we did but love God as well as a
> worldly man doth love his wealth and riches,
> we should be so taken up with the love of God
> as quite to forget the world; for the world
> makes them forget God, that He is not always
> in their thoughts. Yea, we should be taken up
> always with God.

My brethren, what shall we say to this? How shall
we excuse this, that we should be so unmindful of
God while the worldling is so mindful of the world?
Oh, what a shame is this! For shame, be ashamed of
yourselves before we go away hence. I profess,
Christians, I have wondered that God will throw
away His kingdom upon some who care so little for
it as we do. Oh, shame yourself out of this evil frame!

Brethren, why do we not behave towards the
world as the world does toward us? Why should we
not act more strangely towards it? Oh, never leave
until the thoughts of heaven are your natural
thoughts! Oh, check your heart roundly in the
evening for this sin if you find your heart faulty
here, and never leave until you have brought it into
a right frame.

3. Have I been often looking into my heart, and
made conscience even of vain thoughts? You know
your rule: "Keep thy heart with all diligence, for out
of it are the issues of life" (Proverbs 4:23). Now, have

you been keeping your heart with all diligence? Brethren, you may be sure your work will go badly unless you look to your hearts and keep them.

Examine them in the evening. How has my heart been employed today? Has it not been a thoroughfare of vain thoughts? Of evil imaginations?

I fear many of us make little conscience of this. It may be that you make conscience of vain thoughts in duty, but I fear that few Christians make conscience of vain thoughts at other times. Ah, brethren, you have not known what it is to live the life of Christianity if you do not look to this. This must be mended!

Brethren, what a blessed thing would this be if we had but once attained this frame! If our heart naturally ran into a hollow channel! This is attainable, and many Christians have attained unto it. And, if it is attainable, I think we should never be quiet until we have attained it. Why, Christian, take this rule. Force your heart awhile to it; keep your heart for awhile in its track. Set it some holy subject, some good task, and make it ply its work; and when you have gotten to this point, then by degrees it will be sweet to you. It is not enough to say, "What hurt is there in such vain thoughts?" It is enough that there is no good in them, that there is no profit in them. Yea, there is a great deal of hurt in letting your thoughts run abroad.

My brethren, you do, I believe, every one of you who are Christians indeed, complain of the burden of your vain thoughts. I believe that this is the greatest trouble of many Christians here, the vanity of their thoughts in holy duties. And what is the reason for this? Because they let out their hearts at other times. This is the reason why we have no more command of our hearts in holy duties, because we do not keep them in at other times. God complains of Jerusalem in Jeremiah 4:14 (and may He not complain so of us?), "O Jerusalem, how long shall vain thoughts lodge within thee?" Have we not, many of us, been complaining these seven or fourteen years of vain thoughts, and yet they are lodging in us? And if you take this course with your hearts, you will find more benefit in it than ever you did in anything that you have tried hitherto.

But I know what the flesh will say here. "What, to be *always* taken up with holy things? This will be an intolerable burden." Oh, but do not hearken to the evil report that the flesh will bring upon the ways of God. Indeed, I confess, it will bring some difficulty; yet I trust you will be willing to be at some pain for so great a good as this is. After a while, you will find it easy. No trade or foreign language is easy to a learner, but after a little while he becomes used to it and it is his delight. And so will this be the sweetest thing in the world to you, if you keep the heart to it awhile. Therefore, never stop watching and praying until you have gotten the heart into this frame.

4. Have not I given way to the working of pride or passion today? My brethren, the Spirit of God is a holy dove that will not rest in an unquiet and froward heart. It was said by a very holy man, "Whatever you do, take heed of passion." In 2 Kings 3:15, Elisha had to call for a minstrel before he could allay his passion. I beseech you to watch your hearts when there is a temptation to pride and a provo-

cation to passion before you, or else you will grieve the good Spirit of God and make Him to withdraw Himself from you. It is a saying of Mr. Baxter, "When there is a temptation to pride before me, I am careful to watch my heart as narrowly as I would the thatch of my house when fire is put to it; and immediately to throw on it the water of detestation, resolution, and recourse to God." And so must you do if ever you mean to attain to a heavenly heart.

I remember it is written in the life of a holy man that he feared and trembled more when he heard himself commended than when it thundered ever so dreadfully. This frame should be in you. O fear temptations to pride. I beseech you to take heed of pride, that your hearts do not grow haughty. If you do not take good heed, you are likely to fall.

That servant is never likely to do much for God who is puffed up with pride. If you have gotten yourself down and trodden upon the neck of pride, then you have become a great victor indeed. This is the reason why God does not employ us in His service more, because He sees that there is such an evil heart in us that we would make His mercies fuel for our pride and lust. Let it be your daily practice to get the victory over this enemy, the pride of your heart.

Another holy man has set a very exemplary pattern before us. He said, concerning himself, "I think I am broken all in pieces before God when I speak to Him, as when I tread upon an egg and trample it all to pieces." In one of his letters, he wrote to comfort another, "I pray God make use of me, a poor creature, to do you some good." Let us lay this pattern before us. But more especially, look to our holy and humble Jesus and you shall find rest for your souls. Follow your pride and passion thus with observation and detestation every day, and this will wear it out at last.

Fourth, regarding your tongues, ask these questions:

1. Have I bridled my tongue and forced it in? This is a very necessary question that must be inquired into. I tell you, if you have no measure to bridle your tongue, you are no Christian (James 1:26). On the other hand, if you have once gotten this skill to govern your tongue, you are a grown Christian (James 3:2). He who can govern his tongue has attained to some good growth and good perfection in grace. Brethren, you need to set up David's resolution daily from Psalm 39:1: "I said, 'I will take heed to my ways, that I offend not with my tongue.'" Psalm 17:3: "I am purposed that my mouth shall not transgress." And distrusting his own strength, you may see how he runs to God for strength. Psalm 141:3: "Set a watch, O Lord, before my mouth; keep the door of my lips."

2. Have I spoken evil of any man? This is an express charge of the Apostle in Titus 3:1–2: "Put them in mind to speak evil of no man." And the apostle Peter charges us that if we will grow in grace, we must put away evil speaking. This is a great and universal sin among us, that we are apt to speak evil of others. When we hear of anything that is evil in anyone, how do we speak of it to our friends? See that you have good ends and a lawful call to tell before you tell of another's evil. Brethren, it cannot be

sufficiently bewailed that there should be so great an evil among us, that we should be so backward to speak of our brother's evil to himself and so prone to publish it to those that we should not.

3. Has the law of God been in my mouth as I sat in my house and went by the way, lying down, rising up? How great is the charge of God given to us! And how great is our negligence in this work! Deuteronomy 6:7: "Thou shalt teach them diligently unto thy children, and shalt talk of them when thou sittest in thy house, and when thou walkest by the way, and when thou liest down, and when thou risest up." Christian, can your heart acquit you here now? Can your family acquit you, that this is your work when you are sitting by the fire with them? Can your yoke-fellow witness for you that the word of God is in your mouth when you lie down and rise up? Can your fellow-traveler say that these are your talks when you walk? What benefit would this be to others if you did this! When will you come to the full resolution of this? Well, set this resolution with yourself, that you will not let your conscience alone until you come to this.

4. Have I come into no company but I have dropped something of God there, and left some good favor behind? Oh, what a shame is it that Christians should be so unlike themselves that, when they come into company, it cannot be seen who is the Christian and who is not! Oh, how should we be ashamed of this, that we should be ashamed of our God! Oh, that you would make conscience not to come into any company but to drop something of God there.

Fifth, here are questions for your tables.

1. Did I not sit down with no higher end than a beast, merely to please my appetites? Did I eat and drink for the glory of God? You cannot know what it is to be a Christian until you come to do all things by rule. Make conscience of this, to set your ends right when you sit down to your tables.

Is it not a shame that a Christian should sit down with no higher end than a beast to his meat? Beasts eat and drink to satisfy their hunger. Remember that you sit down with an eye upon God. This will make your table to be sanctified to you.

2. Did I not rise from my table without dropping something of God there? Christian, how often do you contradict the example of your Savior? You shall find His discourse, when He sat at the table, that He was always speaking of God. And is it not a shame that you should imitate your Savior no better?

3. Did not my appetite overcome me? Brethren, I fear many of us are little skilled in the duty of temperance. It may be that many of us think we may eat as long as it is pleasing to our appetites. This is a great (though, I fear, a common) evil that, as Jude said, "they feast without fear." Here observe the general rule. Never sit down to your table without using some self-denial. We cannot give an exact rule to everyone, but healthy bodies should eat at one meal so that they may be hungry at the next one. I am verily afraid that this sin of gluttony is a very common sin. Therefore, Christian, set a special watch upon your appetite.

There are two sorts of temperance that we should be aware of, either with respect to the quantity or to the quality of what we eat. We offend in the first when we eat more than we can digest. We offend in the other when a man gives himself to eat what the physician tells him is not fit for him. And what a shame is this that neither reason nor grace should keep a person from breaking out into temperance.

4. Did I not mock God when I pretended to crave a blessing and return thanks? If I may judge by my own experience, I think that we are more formal in this than in any other thing. Well, let this be amended by us. It is a sad thing that we should mock God when we pretend to serve Him.

Sixth, here are four questions regarding your callings.

1. Have I been diligent in the duties of my calling?

2. Have I defrauded any man? Have I observed that golden rule of justice in my dealings this day, that I have done nothing to any man other than what I would have done unto me? When I have considered it, I find that there is more of Christianity in our moral duties than we are aware of. This is not to be a Christian, to be so only in prayer, hearing, and so forth; but to be a Christian in your shops and fields. If you are no second table-man, if you ignore the second table of the law, you are no Christian. Remember that this is to be a reproach to religion.

3. Have I ever dropped a lie in my shop or trade? You who have dealings in the world, you need to look to this every hour. I beseech you, Christians, look to this. This is a fearful sin, and it is a sign that there is nothing of Christianity in you if this pre-

vails. Therefore, set a guard upon your mouth, and beg God to keep your mouth that nothing will come from it but truth. And in the evening, examine how you have kept your charge in this respect.

4. Did I not rashly make or falsely break some promise? There is a great and reigning evil in this respect among those who trade in the world. Be very wary and very sparing in making a promise; and, when you have made it, be sure to perform it. I wonder how else you can read Psalm 15, which says of those who shall enter into the holy hill of the Lord that "he sweareth to his own hurt and performeth it."

CONCLUSION. And thus I have given you materials for the examining of your own hearts. Now, my further business to you is to know your resolve to perform this. Will you content yourselves with the approving of these rules only, or will you apply them in practice? I beseech you, do not rest in bare resolution and intention, but resolve that never a day shall pass before you do these things.

To stir you up hereunto, let me give you these three motives.

First, consider that there will be no such means in the world for you to get a sound and thorough conquest over your corruptions. You have been striving a great while with your corruptions—some with vain thoughts, some with pride, some with passion—and it may be that you have gotten but little victory. And what is the reason? Because you have not followed the battle with constancy. If you took your heart to task every day about it, you would surely get the victory over it.

A holy man, much experienced in this area, made the following comparison: "You must watch your corruptions as a cat does her prey; either it must stay in, or else she has it." If you did this, you would quickly find the thief, and so would bring it to the bar beforehand and have execution carried out upon it. We must daily be in pursuit of our corruptions; we must never give over the chase, not in one prayer or one day, and then we are likely to get the victory over it.

Second, consider this is a ready way to assurance. Brethren, the great reason why Christians are without assurance is for lack of self-examination, for lack of pain and diligence in observing their own heart. But now, if you set upon this duty, you will be skilled in knowing your own hearts. I believe this work of self-examination is seldom done by many Christians unless it is upon some special occasion.

Third, consider hereby you shall come to a thorough acquaintance with your own hearts. 2 Corinthians 13:5: "Prove yourselves"; and then follows, "Know you yourselves?" He who proves himself often shall know himself at length.

The Fruit and Benefit of Worthy Receiving

by Richard Vines

There is great benefit of this sacrament to those who commune therein preparedly, though all are not agreed what the benefit is, as may be seen by the doctrine of the papist, the Socinian, and the Orthodox. That there *is* a benefit, few will deny; and if it is denied, the sensible experience of many godly Christians attests it, to which experience the Apostle sometimes appeals. Galatians 3:2: "This only would I learn of you." And for others who will not own their experiences, or do not have them, reason may convince them that as God made no useless creature, so He ordains no fruitless institutions. This ordinance was instituted for the use of His select people, and that was done at such a time as our Lord had the very powers of darkness to encounter; therefore it is an ordinance of some moment, which began at the death, and stands in force until the second coming, of Christ. And if nothing else is said, this is enough: the guilt and danger of receiving unworthily are so dreadful that there must in reason be some proportion of benefit and fruit related to worthy receiving, which reason may convince any rational man that there is not only a good, but that good is of very great proportion and degree, and that you shall not come for fruit to a barren fig tree.

I have reason to demonstrate these two points:
1. There is a benefit.
2. What that benefit is.

1. There is much benefit by worthy receiving of the Lord's Supper.

Lest this sacrament of so great moment be vilified and brought to contempt, like a dry teat or an empty vessel, people must neglect both the use of this sacrament and all preparation thereunto who undervalue it as fruitless and not beneficial. Who will take any pains to go to a dry well that has no water in it? It's vain to urge preparations on those who are not persuaded of any benefit in it. And though I will not dispute whether the supreme Lord may not oblige His creature, man, for probation and trial of his obedience to a duty whence no other benefit should redound but the very duty of obedience, as He obliged Abraham by a law to sacrifice his son, yet I conceive that God's standing ordinances and laws not only oblige a duty, but intend a benefit, and thereby invite obedience. It is said in Deuteronomy 10:12–13: "What doth the Lord require of thee, but to keep His commandments for thy good?" And therefore there is a benefit of the right use of this sacrament, by which we may lawfully be excited and impelled to observe the ordinance as we climb the tree for the fruit that is upon it. It's true, an unworthy communicant reaps no other benefit than something like that which the Apostle calls the advantage and profit of the Jews (Romans 3:1 and 9:4), the tables and seals of the covenant; but the reason why he receives no inward and spiritual fruit is not that

there is no water in this well, but that he has no
bucket to draw it forth. For God offers and holds
forth Christ and the benefits of the covenant. His
hand is not empty, but ours is so full of sin and self-
righteousness that we cannot receive it, for those
who will receive must bring some capacity to do so.
It's a known truth: he who means to receive a benefit which is conveyed by way of covenant must bring
the condition of that covenant in his hand, just as
he who comes to a table must bring life and stomach.

I know there are some godly ones who fear, or
perhaps will boldly affirm, that they were never sensible of the benefit of this sacrament. They hear of
good fruit, but they have not tasted it; and therefore
their edge is dull and flat as to the receiving of it. To
that I answer this: if there is an exercise of the
graces required in the act of receiving, they may not
deny the fruit of the ordinance because it is not so
clearly sensible at the present, for, perhaps, they
limit God to the present time or confine their expectations to some particular fruit, such as elevation
of heart, sensible comfort, clear assurance, or the
like, which, because they find not, they think they
have nothing.

God answers the expectations and satisfies the
necessity of His people by giving some other grace
than we would have, or have our eye upon. Paul's
prayers were answered in sufficient grace, not in the
removing of the thorn. We cry for comfortable
signs, and God gives obediential and serviceable
graces. We look for spiritual gifts, and He gives
humbling grace. We would have conquest of sin,

and God gives power to encounter it. We look for lively grace, and God keeps grace alive. We expect at present, and God afterward gives us it.

In bodily nourishment, it's not possible for a man to tell what degree of nourishment he received by a particular meal, yet he finds that he lives and is strengthened, and he may be nourished by that which he does not relish with delight. As for those who, upon pretense of spirit and spirituality, have cast off ordinances as fruitless, I would wish they would consider whether they are not rather beside their wits than above ordinances, seeing Christ Himself—not only by His institution, but by His example—commends this sacrament unto us as a standing ordinance for the whole church "until He comes." And so He has commanded the ministry also "till we all come to a full stature" (Ephesians 4:13). I would like to know how that spirit which has carried them to the pinnacle of the temple, and has set them above ordinances, or which witnesses to them without graces, can be proven to be the Spirit of Christ. And if they would show us how they can live without meat and drink too, there would be some hope that they might be starved into their senses and right minds.

So much for the first point, that there is a fruit and benefit from this ordinance.

2. What that benefit is.

I have reason to show what it is because carnal and superstitious persons expect what they have no warrant to expect, perverting the use of this sacrament to other intents and ends than it has by insti-

tution of Christ. The sick man too superstitiously
conceives that the act of communion is a token that
will pay his fare into heaven, or that is like a popish
shrift that blots out all sin and wipes off the old
score. If instead of making the right use we idolize
the brazen serpent and worship it, what is it but superstition? The only way to avoid that is to mind the
institution and the end thereof, or else we shall look
for that which God never intended to convey, as Eve
was deceived in the fruit of the tree of which she ate.

I will show what the benefit is because men commonly have confused thoughts that there is a benefit, but they know not what. They think it's good for
something, but they know not what, and so they, as
it were, take medicine merely upon trust, not knowing what it is. Hence is that awfulness of this ordinance with all men. They must be holy now at this
time. They must not follow their wicked and loose
ways. They are going to the sacrament, and they go
with an ignorant reverence, not knowing either the
fruit or the danger of it.

What is the effect, as some call it, or the fruit and
benefit of this sacrament? I will answer generally,
and then more particularly.

1. The benefit of the sacrament is of a higher nature than these creatures are able to convey, and
therefore they are stamped and made instrumental
by an institution of God. It would have been both
vain and superstitious to have expected spiritual
benefit by the use of these elements had not the
word of institution given a new relation to them,
which, without it, they do not have. A similitude or
representation might have been borrowed to signify

the sufferings of Christ, but that would not have
made a sacrament any more than marriage, repre-
senting the mystical union of Christ and the
Church, is therefore a sacrament. There must be a
promise and a command of God added to the visible
creature whereby the use of it to such a purpose is
warranted and authorized. Therefore we must look
higher than the outward elements or their power.
An axe is more than iron; a seal is more than wax.
God's institution renders the creatures of bread and
wine (as Bellarmine notes, though two elements are
but one instrument or seal) useful to spiritual ef-
fects, not by elevating their natures—as the iron or
wax, being physical instruments, are not elevated to
any efficacy in themselves—but by appointing their
use and working by them. Therefore that question
of how bread and wine reach or touch the soul is
impertinent. For it refers to a natural conclusion;
but moral relation needs no contact. There is a benefit that follows the right use of them, which comes
not through them as through a conduit, but from
God by the use of such means, as an estate is conveyed from the donor by a seal of wax.

2. The benefits and blessings promised in the
covenant of grace are sealed, and the graces of the
covenant are improved in a believer, by this ordinance: Christ, Christ crucified, or rather in crucifying, together with such benefits as are immediately
sealed in His death (reconciliation, redemption,
remission of sins), as on God's part offered to a sinner, are here signed and sealed. And faith in Christ
and repentance from dead works are here exercised,
excited, confirmed, and renewed: the main funda-

mental and essential benefits and graces which are in most necessary order to salvation, are here reinforced, not such things as some Christians have and some do not, but the common necessities of the covenant, both on God's part and ours, without which no Christian can be saved.

Therefore I cannot help but wonder that many well-meaning souls should fix their eyes on such benefits or gifts to be given in this sacrament as are not common to all, but are eminencies of some and not of all. They look for gifts of prayer, of memory, freedom from passions, some parts or endowments which they see others excel in, and if they do not gain these, they think they gain nothing, as if they were unworthy. Alas, that you should so err!

I tell you, covenant benefits, covenant graces, the roots and the vitals, these are what receive improvement here. Here Christ is offered and faith is quickened. Here Christ crucified is exhibited and here repentance is renewed. These are the main benefits that God can give, the main graces that we can have, such as are essential, without which salvation is nonexistent. This I would have observed for the honor of the ordinance, and the quickening of your approach to it.

And another thing also: when you hear us use the words "exhibit," "convey," "confer," "afford grace," or "spiritual benefits," you should understand that this is not as a natural agent, but in a way proper to a sacrament. As we say, an estate passes by the seal; that is, it is assured or confirmed, or, as we say, the promise or contract passes by a ring. These are words which everyone understands. And doubtless the benefit and fruit of the sacrament is afforded in a particular way.

As the Word, besides begetting grace, also increases and confirms, but not in the same way as the sacrament does; as it may be the same bargain that passes by promise, by oath, by earnest, or by seal, as these are several ways of certification; so it's the same grace that is nourished by the sacrament as by the Word, but the way is different. That of the sacrament is by way of sign and seal; that of the Word by way of promise or covenant agreement. Nay, the two sacraments themselves differ in their properties: baptism seals the covenant by way of initiation, and the Lord's Supper does it by way of nutrition or augmentation. God did not make or multiply ordinances at random without their distinct and particular use for exhibiting to us the same Christ, the same graces, the same benefits, as men have several ways of making assurance one to another.

We have dealt with the generalities; now, for the particular, let us consider what is here done and what is hence received. There are here done two things by Christ, and, answerably, there are two things done by a believer in Christ.

Two things principally are here done by God or by Christ: First, Christ crucified is really exhibited to the faith of a believer; second, the gracious covenant which God has made in Christ is sealed to a believer.

1. Christ crucified, together with all those benefits that ensue upon His death, is really exhibited to a believer. For there is not a mere representation or empty figure, but a real and true exhibition of Christ

Himself as broken for our sins. The words translated "take ye, eat ye" evidently confirm it to us. If there were only a resemblance or figurative representation, then "see ye" would have been more properly said. But "Take, eat, this is My body" plainly shows that Christ Himself is here given to a believer. I think we look so much on the representation that we forget the exhibition, and therefore should labor to conclude that Christ Himself, as in the state of a redeeming Savior, is truly and indeed held forth and presented to our faith as verily as any benefit can be offered and held forth by one man to another. This body and blood were really offered up to God for us, which in this sacrament are really offered and applied to us by faith.

Answerable to this exhibition of Christ Himself, the believer performs an act of communion (1 Corinthians 10:16), partaking of the body and blood of Christ in a spiritual sense for spiritual nourishment, to increase and build up. For the new creature is fed and maintained by Christ, and by virtue of union with Him we have communion, as the vine branches, by their union with the vine, receive sap and nourishment. We have no graces or benefits without Christ, but first in order of nature we have union as members of Him, and then of His fullness we receive. For a Christian is like a branch that has nothing of its own but what it receives from the root; as it springs from the root, so its increase and growth is from the root also. He is as the moon which, as it appears in the eclipse, has no light of itself, but increases and comes to fullness as it receives from the sun.

Let no man think that a believer has no further use of Christ after his first believing and receiving of Him, for then this sacrament would not be useful; the effect whereof, as Durand said, is not absolutely necessary to salvation, as if one could not be in a state of salvation without it, because it serves for confirmation of one who is already in a saved state. And it's plain that a great part of Christ's office is exercised in preserving and continuing them in Him who are already members of Him. Therefore He is the Finisher of our faith as well as the Author of our faith, for we live in Him and from Him, and our grace is maintained by continual emanations from the Son. And therefore this ordinance of communion with Christ, and the exercise of such acts of communion, are of prime use and benefit, as the branch that shoots from the tree grows and lives from that root which gave to it the first being by a contrived influx of sap into it. And this is the first combination of God's act and of ours.

2. The second combination is this: the gracious covenant which God has made in Christ is sealed to a believer. The communion nature of a sacrament is to be a seal of justification or righteousness with God by faith in Christ (Romans 4:11). As a seal refers to some covenant, so the sacrament refers to God's covenant with man, which is this: God promises to accept into favor and into His propriety all who believe in and receive Christ, and to bestow upon them all the blessings and benefits thereof. God gives Christ by way of covenant. He covenants with Christ our Lord that He should "give His soul an offering and a sacrifice for sin, and in so doing should see

His seed" (Isaiah 53:10). So Arminius, in *this* point, at least, is orthodox. Of this covenant, the death or blood of Christ is the condition which Christ accepted and performed.

The covenant of God with us is that all who believe in Christ who died, and receive Him as their Lord and Savior, shall have remission of sins, and of this covenant the blood of Christ is the ratification, as the testator's death ratifies the will or testament. For it is blood that dedicates the testament (Hebrews 9:18), and so in the words, "This cup is the new testament (or covenant) in My blood," dedicated thereby; and we receive this blood in this sacrament as the seal of the gracious covenant made with us. So if doubts arise concerning the reality of God and the sureness of this covenant that speaks of so much grace and mercy, we look upon and take hold of this seal of blood, and are thereby settled and therein acquiesce.

Answerable to this act of God, the believer accepts and submits to this covenant and the conditions of it, which are to believe and to have God for our God; and thereof he makes a solemn profession in this sacrament, giving himself up to Christ as Lord and Savior, recommitting himself to be His. So he binds himself and, as it were, seals a counterpart to God again; and not only so, but he comes into a claim of all the riches and legacies of the will or covenant because he has accepted, and here declares his acceptance of, the covenant. The seal is indeed properly of that which is God's part of the covenant to perform and give, but it is only offered until we subscribe and set our hands to it. Then it becomes complete and the benefits may be claimed, as the benefit of any conditional promise may be when the condition is performed.

And, lest you should stumble at that word, I must let you know that the will's accepting and submitting to the conditions is the performance of the conditions required, and so the gracious God who might require duty and allegiance of His creature condescends to enter into a covenant of grace with us, and vouchsafes the honor of coming into covenant with Him so that He might settle and maintain a communion and correspondence between Himself and His people, and that there might be a mutual bond of engagement to each other. This is solemnly professed as often as we meet with God in this sacrament, because we are so apt to disbelieve and waver about His promises, and to halt and decline from our obligations to Him. And this is the second combination of action, according to that which is to be remembered at every sealing day (the sacrament is a sealing day). Deuteronomy 26:17–18: "Thou hast avouched the Lord this day to be thy God, and to walk in His ways. And the Lord hath avouched thee to be His peculiar people, as He hath promised thee."

I come to the second point, that of what is here received. I do not mean to say what every believer sensibly receives, but what God has appointed by this sacrament to convey, and what may be received by a believer in the right use of it, not always in his own sense, but according to the nature of this ordinance.

I will not say that which some affirm (but is really apocryphal) of the manna which the Israelites ate, that it had the taste that every man desired. But this I will say, which Calvin said of himself: "When I have said all, I have said little; the tongue is overcome, yea, the mind is overwhelmed."

I say, then, Christ is here received into intimate union, the body and blood of the Lord, as the nourishment of our souls. What is more ours than the meat we eat? What is more nearly joined to us than that which becomes part of ourselves?

The Scripture, by the language it uses, has even overcome our apprehensions. A man may eat the fruit that has no interest in the tree, but here the believing eater grows into the tree. He who drinks, drinks the fountain; he comes to a closer union with the conduit pipe of all grace, the flesh of Jesus Christ. You know the best meat and drink does you no good unless it is made your own; nor is Christ of any worth unless He is ours. He is as if He were not. We must be happy by having Christ within us. "Know you not that Christ is in you, except you be reprobates?" (2 Corinthians 13:5). There was a crowd that touched Christ, but "virtue went out of Him to none but one" who touched Him by faith. So there is a throng about the table, but none receive Christ except those who by faith take and eat His crucified body. If Christ Himself is here received, what spiritual grace is there that is not in Him?

It is somewhat a gross conceit to ask how Christ in heaven and a believer on earth can be united. For man and wife are one flesh though a thousand miles apart. And we know that, as the Apostle says, "there are bands and joints whereby the head and every member, the root and every branch are united" (Colossians 2:19), and they in this mystical union are Spirit and faith. "He that is joined to the Lord is one spirit" (1 Corinthians 6:17). And so, according to that strange expression, "We are members of His body, of His flesh, and of His bones" (Ephesians 5:30). This phrase signifies that the human nature of Christ is the root of this union, but this union must not be distorted by too subtle curiosity because it is mystical.

A believer in Christ may here receive remission of sin, not venial only (as papists teach), but deadly and mortal sins as well. Oh, but may we truly come with such sins? Yes, with repentance and remorse for them. We may bring our sins to the Head of our sacrifice, and put them thereupon by confession. Bellarmine resolves all the differences between papists and Protestants about the effect of this sacrament into this: the papists deny that the Protestants hold remission of sin to be given here, and the papists do it in favor of their sacrament of penance so that one sacrament may not rob another. But Scripture tells us: "This is My blood of the new testament which is shed for many for remission of sins" (Matthew 26:28). Shed for remission, that's true, says Bellarmine, but not given in the sacrament—a mere evasion, for we drink the blood that was shed, even that which confirms the new testament, which promises remission of sin. The great argument wherein a believer triumphs before his final victory is that he has remission of sin before he comes by his faith in Christ, and that's true. But in this sacrament the pardon passes before a believer is pardoned by the covenant, and here that pardon is sealed, and sealed it cannot be unless it is before; for the pardon of forgiven sins is sealed, as "Abraham received the sign of circumcision, the seal of the righteousness of faith, which he had before" (Romans 4:11).

And this is needful for relief of our doubts, fears, and waverings; for this is the great question of anxiety which troubles the soul: Are my sins pardoned? Are my sins blotted out? And God has, according to Chemnitz, instituted this sacrament to resolve this question for the weak in faith. Behold the seal; believe upon the Word, believe upon the seal of God.

Luther explains it by a gradation: "the cup is put for the wine; the wine signifies the blood; 'the blood is the blood of the new testament' " (Matthew 26:28). The new testament contains the gracious pardon of sin to a believer, and if remission of sin is an article of the covenant, the scale must reach it. Therefore, all who have wounded their souls with grievous sins are wounded again with sorrow; they put off the intention to sin and bring repentance and faith; they touch the hem of Christ, receive here the pardon of sin, and question not the seal or truth of it.

That I may not divide into further particulars, there is by this sacrament a communication of a greater proportion of gospel spirit, "for we have been all made to drink into one Spirit" (1 Corinthians 12:13). This Spirit plentifully bestows His several fruits and graces so that a member may grow up into Christ, the Head in all things (Ephesians 4:15), from whence we have those actual influences and

aids of delight, comfort, evidence, sweet tastes, powerful motions and impressions, which Vasquez calls
"grace sacramental," though he says that sacramental grace is not habitual grace but actual influences,
which I think is an error. For though a man has a
sweet taste and transient delight in meat or wine, yet
there is also a permanent and abiding nourishment
proceeding from what he eats or drinks. So here the
very habitual graces are nourished, strengthened,
and excited.

It may be that a man at present does not feel that
strength he receives, nor is sensible of the intention
of his graces. But the growth of grace manifests itself in time. We do not see ourselves or others grow,
but that we have grown is plain enough. We do not
see how much the light increases by every step of the
sun rising higher, for its growth is gradual and by
imperceptible instances and degrees. Similarly,
when our power to resist temptations and mortify
lusts, which before were too hard for us, appears, we
may see our growth, just as we may see our shadows
shortened, but how much it happens in a minute we
may not see.

And we may say that the graces which this ordinance requires and excites are thereby strengthened
and enlarged, and therefore the rule is good: what
grace you would have strengthened by this ordinance, that set to work on and exercise, for that is
"sowing to the Spirit," as the Apostle calls it. And I
have no doubt that a believer shall find the benefit
of this sacrament in his obedience also, for the
fuller the vessel is, the faster it will run out at the
tap. If the habits increase, the fruit of obedience will

be proportionate. We mend a barren tree at the root and sweeten the sap there, and the tree is more fruitful. When Jacob had seen the sweet vision in Bethel, then he continued on his journey (Genesis 29:1). It put mettle into him.

So much for this point, the benefit of this sacrament, which, being diffused, as at this time, is a great loss to the improvement of Christians, though they do not see it. The Christians in times of persecution, when a storm was coming, then were most diligent to frequent this table, to lay in store for a hard winter and fortify their resolutions. And let this benefit be a motive to the use of preparation, which was the reason I have handled it in this place, for there is no promise nor benefit to one who comes to this table unworthily.

The Mystery of the Lord's Supper

by Thomas Watson

"And as they were eating, Jesus took bread, and blessed it, and brake it, and gave it to the disciples, and said, 'Take, eat; this is My body.' And He took the cup, and gave thanks, and gave it to them saying, 'Drink ye all of it; for this is My blood of the new testament, which is shed for many for the remission of sins.' " Matthew 26:26–28

In these words, we have the institution of the Lord's Supper. The Greeks call the sacrament "a mystery." There is in it a mystery of wonder and a mystery of mercy. "The celebration of the Lord's Supper," said Chrysostom, "is the commemoration of the greatest blessing that ever the world enjoyed." A sacrament is a visible sermon. And herein the sacrament excels the Word preached. The Word is a trumpet to proclaim Christ. The sacrament is a glass to represent Him.

QUESTION. But why was the sacrament of the Lord's Supper appointed? Is not the Word sufficient to bring us to heaven?

ANSWER. The Word is for the engrafting; the sacraments are for the confirming of faith. The Word brings us to Christ; the sacrament builds us up in Him. The Word is the font where we are baptized with the Holy Ghost; the sacrament is the table where we are fed and cherished. The Lord condescends to our weakness. Were we made up all of spirit, there would be no need of bread and wine. But we are compounded creatures. Therefore God, to help our faith, not only gives us an audible word but a visible sign. I may here allude to that saying of our Savior, "Except ye see signs, ye will not believe" (John 4:48). Christ sets His body and blood before us in the elements. Here are signs, else we will not believe.

Things taken in by the eye work more upon us than things taken in by the ear. A solemn spectacle of mortality more affects us than an oration. So, when we see Christ broken in the bread and, as it were, crucified before us, this more affects our hearts than the bare preaching of the Word.

So I come to the text. "As they were eating, Jesus took bread." Where I shall open these five particulars in reference to the sacrament:

1. The Author.
2. The Time.
3. The Manner.
4. The Guests.
5. The Benefits.

1. The Author of the sacrament, Jesus Christ. "Jesus took bread." To institute sacraments belongs, by right, to Christ, and is a flower of His crown. He only who can give grace can appoint the sacraments, which are the seals of grace. Christ, being the Founder of the sacrament, gives a glory and luster to it. A king making a feast adds more state and magnificence to it. "Jesus took bread," He whose name is above every name, God blessed forever (Philippians 2:9).

2. The time when Christ instituted the sacrament; wherein we may take notice of two circumstances:

1. *It was when He had supped;* "after supper" (Luke 22:20,) which had this mystery in it, to show that the sacrament is chiefly intended as a spiritual banquet. It was not to indulge the senses, but to feast the graces. It was "after supper."

2. *The other circumstance of time is that Christ appointed the sacrament a little before His sufferings.* "The Lord Jesus, the same night in which He was betrayed, took bread" (1 Corinthians 11:23). He knew troubles were now coming upon His disciples. It would be no small perplexity to them to see their Lord and Master crucified. And shortly after they must pledge Him in a bitter cup. Therefore, to arm them against such a time and to animate their spirits, that very night in which He was betrayed He gives them His body and blood in the sacrament.

This may give us a good hint that, in all trouble of mind, especially approaches of danger, it is needful to have recourse to the Lord's Supper. The sacrament is both an antidote against fear and a restorative to faith. The night in which Christ was betrayed, He took bread.

3. The manner of the institution; wherein four things are observable: (1) The taking of the bread; (2) The breaking of it; (3) The blessing of it; and (4) The administering of the cup.

1. *The taking of the bread.* "Jesus took bread."

QUESTION. What is meant by this phrase, "He took bread?"

ANSWER. Christ's taking and separating the bread from common uses holds forth a double mystery.

First, it signified that God in His eternal decree set Christ apart for the work of our redemption. He was separate from sinners (Hebrews 7:26).

Second, Christ's setting the elements apart from common bread and wine showed that He is not for common persons to feed upon. They are to be divinely purified who touch these holy things of God. They must be outwardly separated from the world and inwardly sanctified by the Spirit.

QUESTION. Why did Christ take bread rather than any other element?

ANSWER 1. Because it prefigured Him. Christ was typified by the show-bread (1 Kings 7:48); by the bread which Melchizedek offered unto Abraham (Genesis 14:18); and by the cake which the angel brought to Elijah (1 Kings 19:6). Therefore, He took bread to answer the type.

ANSWER 2. Christ took bread because of the analogy. Bread resembled Him closely. "I am that Bread of life" (John 6:48). There is a three-fold resemblance:

Bread is useful. Other comforts are more for delight than use. Music delights the ear, colors the eye, but bread is the staff of life. So Christ is useful. There is no subsisting without Him. "He that eateth Me, even he shall live by Me" (John 6:57).

Bread is satisfying. If a man is hungry, flowers or pictures do not satisfy, but bread does. So Jesus

Christ, the Bread of the soul, satisfies. He satisfies the eye with beauty, the heart with sweetness, the conscience with peace.

Bread is strengthening. "Bread which strengthens man's heart" (Psalm 104:15). So Christ, the Bread of the soul, transmits strength. He strengthens us against temptations and for doing and suffering work. He is like the cake the angel brought to the prophet. "He arose and did eat, and went in the strength of that meat forty days and forty nights, unto Horeb the mount of God" (1 Kings 19:8).

2. *The second thing in the institution is the breaking of the bread.* "He brake it." This shadowed out Christ's death and passion with all the torments of His body and soul. "It pleased the Lord to bruise Him" (Isaiah 53:10). When the spices are bruised, then they send forth a sweet savor. So, when Christ was bruised on the cross, He sent out a fragrant smell. Christ's body crucifying was the breaking open of a box of precious ointment which filled heaven and earth with its perfume.

QUESTION. But why was Christ's body broken? What was the cause of His suffering?

ANSWER. Surely not for any desert of His own. "The Messiah shall be cut off, but not for Himself" (Daniel 9:26). In the original it is, "He shall be cut off, and there is nothing in Him." There is no cause in Him why He should suffer. When the high priest went into the tabernacle, offered first "for himself" (Hebrews 9:7). Though he had his mitre or golden plate, and wore holy garments, yet he was not pure and innocent. He must offer sacrifice for himself as well as the people. But Jesus Christ, that great High

Priest, though He offered a bloody sacrifice, yet it was not for Himself.

Why, then, was His blessed body broken? It was for our sins. "He was wounded for our transgressions" (Isaiah 53:5). The Hebrew word for "wounded" has a double emphasis. Either it may signify that He was pierced through as with a dart, or that He was profaned. He was used as some common vile thing, and Christ can thank us for it. "He was wounded for our transgressions." So that, if the question were put to us, as once was put to Christ, "Prophesy, who smote Thee?" (Luke 22:64), we might soon answer that it was our sins that smote Him. Our pride made Christ wear a crown of thorns. As Zipporah said to Moses, "A bloody husband art thou to me" (Exodus 4:25), so may Christ say to His church, "A bloody spouse you have been to Me; you have cost Me My heart's blood."

QUESTION. But how could Christ suffer, being God? The Godhead is impassible.

ANSWER. Christ suffered only in the human nature, not the divine. Damascen expresses it by this simile: If one pours water on iron that is red hot, the fire suffers by the water and is extinguished; but the iron does not suffer. So the human nature of Christ might suffer death, but the divine nature is not capable of any passion. When Christ was in the human nature, He was in the divine nature triumphing. As we wonder at the rising of the Son of righteousness in His incarnation, so we may wonder at the going down of this Sun in His passion.

QUESTION. If Christ suffered in His human nature only, how could His suffering satisfy for sin?

ANSWER. By reason of the hypostatic union, the human nature being united to the divine. The human nature suffered; the divine nature satisfied. Christ's Godhead gave both majesty and efficacy to His sufferings. Christ was Sacrifice, Priest, and Altar. He was Sacrifice, as He was man; Priest, as He was God and man; Altar, as He was God. It is the property of the altar to sanctify the thing offered on it (Matthew 23:19). So the altar of Christ's divine nature sanctified the sacrifice of His death and made it meritorious.

Now, concerning Christ's suffering upon the cross, observe these things:

The bitterness of it to Him. "He was broken." The very thoughts of His suffering put Him into an agony. "Being in agony, He prayed more earnestly, and He sweat, as it were, great drops of blood falling down to the ground" (Luke 22:44). He was full of sorrow. "My soul is exceeding sorrowful, even unto death" (Matthew 26:38).

Christ's crucifixion was:

1. A lingering death. It was more for Christ to suffer one hour than for us to have suffered forever. But His death was lengthened out. He hung three hours on the cross. He died many deaths before He could die one.

2. It was a painful death. His hands and feet were nailed, which parts, being full of sinews, and therefore very tender, His pain must be most acute and sharp. And to have the envenomed arrow of God's wrath shot to His heart, this was the direful catastrophe, and caused that outcry upon the cross, "My God, My God, why hast Thou forsaken Me?" The jus-

tice of God was now enflamed and heightened to its
full. "God spared not His Son" (Romans 8:32).
Nothing must be abated of the debt. Christ felt the
pains of hell, though not locally, yet equivalently. In
the sacrament, we see this tragedy acted before us.

3. It was a shameful death. Christ was hung between two thieves (Matthew 27:38). It was as if He
had been the principal malefactor. Well might the
lamp of heaven withdraw its light and mask itself
with darkness, as blushing to behold the Sun of
righteousness in an eclipse. It is hard to say which
was greater, the blood of the cross or the shame of
the cross (Hebrews 12:2).

4. It was a cursed death (Deuteronomy 21:23).
This kind of death was deemed exceedingly execrable, yet the Lord Jesus underwent this, "Being
made a curse for us" (Galatians 3:13). He who was
God blessed forever (Romans 9:5) was under a curse.

Also, consider the sweetness of it to us. Christ's
bruising is our healing. "By His stripes, we are
healed" (Isaiah 53:5). Calvin calls the crucifixion of
Christ the hinge on which our salvation turns.
Luther calls it a gospel spring opened to refresh
sinners. Indeed, the suffering of Christ is a deathbed cordial. It is an antidote to expel all our fear.
Does sin trouble? Christ has overcome it for us.
Besides the two thieves crucified with Christ, there
were two other invisible thieves crucified with Him:
sin and the devil.

3. *The third thing in the institution is Christ's blessing of
the bread.* "He blessed it." This was the consecration
of the elements. Christ, by His blessing, sanctified
them and made them symbols of His body and

blood. Christ's consecrating of the elements points out three things:

Christ, in blessing the elements, opened the nature of the sacrament to the apostles. He explained this mystery. Christ advertised them, that as surely as they received the elements corporeally, so surely they received Him into their hearts spiritually.

Christ's blessing the elements signified His prayer for a blessing upon the ordinance. He prayed that these symbols of bread and wine might, through the blessing and operation of the Holy Ghost, sanctify the elect and seal up all spiritual mercies and privileges to them.

Christ's blessing the elements was His giving thanks. So it is in the Greek, "He gave thanks." Christ gave thanks that God the Father had, in the infinite riches of His grace, given His Son to expiate the sins of the world. And if Christ gave thanks, how may we give thanks! If He gave thanks who was to shed His blood, how may we give thanks who are to drink it! Christ also gave thanks that God had given these elements of bread and wine to not only be signs but seals of our redemption. As the seal serves to make over a conveyance of land, so the sacrament, as a spiritual seal, serves to make over Christ and heaven to such as worthily receive it.

4. *The fourth particular in the institution is Christ's administering the cup.* "And He took the cup." The taking of the cup showed the redundancy of merit in Christ and the copiousness of our redemption. Christ was not sparing. He not only gave us the bread but the cup. We may say as the psalmist, "With the Lord is plenteous redemption" (Psalm 130:7).

If Christ gave the cup, how dare the papists withhold it? They clip and mutilate the ordinance. They plot out Scripture and may fear that doom, "If any man shall take away from the words of the book of this prophecy, God shall take away his part out of the book of life" (Revelation 22:19).

QUESTION. What is meant by Christ's taking the cup?

ANSWER. The cup is figurative; it is a metonymy of the subject. The cup is put for the wine in it. By this, Christ signified the shedding of His blood upon the cross. When His blood was poured out, now the vine was cut and bled. Now was the lily of the valleys dyed a purple color. This was, to Christ, a cup of astonishment (Ezekiel 23:33). But to us, it is a cup of salvation. When Christ drank this cup of blood, we may truly say that He drank a toast to the world. It was precious blood (1 Peter 1:19). In this blood, we see sin fully punished and fully pardoned. Well may the spouse give Christ of her spiced wine and the juice of her pomegranate (Song of Solomon 8:2), when Christ has given her a draft of His warm blood, spiced with His love and perfumed with the divine nature.

4. The fourth thing is the guests invited to this supper, or the persons to whom Christ distributed the elements. "He gave to His disciples and said, 'Take, eat.' " The sacrament is children's bread. If a man makes a feast, he calls his friends. Christ calls His disciples; if He had any piece better than another, He carves it to them.

"This is My body which is given for you" (Luke 22:19), that is, for you believers. Christ gave His body and blood to the disciples chiefly under this notion, that they were believers. As Christ poured out His prayers (John 17:9), so His blood only for believers. See how near to Christ's heart all believers lie! Christ's body was broken on the cross and His blood shed for them. The election has obtained it (Romans 11:7). Christ has passed by others, and died intentionally for them. Impenitent sinners have no benefit by Christ's death unless it is a short reprieve. Christ is given to the wicked in wrath. He is a Rock of offence (1 Peter 2:8). Christ's blood is like chemical drops of oil which recover some patients, but kill others. Judas sucked death from the tree of life. God can turn stones into bread, and a sinner can turn bread into stones—the bread of life into the stone of stumbling.

5. The fifth thing observable in the text is the benefit of this supper in these words, "for the remission of sins." This is a mercy of the first magnitude, the crowning blessing. "Who forgiveth thy iniquities, who crowneth thee with lovingkindness" (Psalm 103:3–4). Whosoever has this charter granted is enrolled in the Book of life. "Blessed is he whose transgression is forgiven" (Psalm 32:1). Under this word, "remission of sin," by a synecdoche, are comprehended all heavenly benedictions, justification, adoption, and glory—in respect of which benefits we may, with Chrysostom, call the Lord's Supper "the feast of the cross."

Application

USE 1. This doctrine of the sacrament confutes the opinion of transubstantiation. When Christ said, "This is My body," the papists affirm that the bread, after the consecration, is turned into the substance of Christ's body. We hold that Christ's body is in the sacrament spiritually. But the papists say that it is there carnally, which opinion is both absurd and impious.

<u>Absurd</u>. For it is contrary, first, to Scripture. The Scripture asserts that Christ's body is locally and numerically in heaven. "Whom the heavens must receive until the times of restitution of all things" (Acts 3:21). If Christ's body is circumscribed in heaven, then it cannot be materially in the eucharist. Second, it is contrary to reason. How is it imaginable that a thing should be changed into another species, yet continue the same? That the bread in the sacrament should be transmuted and turned into flesh, yet remain bread still? When Moses' rod was turned into a serpent, it could not be at the same time both a rod and a serpent. That the bread in the sacrament should be changed into the body of Christ, and yet remain bread, is a perfect contradiction. If the papist says that the bread is vanished, this is more fit to be put into their legend than our creed, for the color, form, and relish of the bread still remains.

<u>Impious</u>. This opinion of transubstantiation is impious, as appears in two things. First, it is a profaning of Christ's body. For if the bread in the sacrament is the real body of Christ, then it may be

eaten not only by the wicked but by reptiles and vermin, which were to disparage and cast contempt upon Christ and His ordinance. Second, it runs men inevitably upon sin. For through this mistake, that the bread is Christ's very body, there follows the divine worship given to the bread—which is idolatry—as also the offering up of the bread, or host, in the mass, which is a blasphemy against Christ's priestly office (Hebrews 10:14), as if His sacrifice on the cross were imperfect.

Therefore, I conclude with Peter Martyr that this doctrine of transubstantiation is to be abhorred and exploded, being minted only in men's fancies but not sprung up in the field of the Holy Scriptures.

Also, this doctrine of the sacrament confutes such as look upon the Lord's Supper only as an empty figure or shadow, resembling Christ's death, but having no intrinsic efficacy in it. Surely, this glorious ordinance is more than an effigy or representative of Christ. Why is the Lord's Supper called the communion of the body of Christ (1 Corinthians 10:16), but because, in the right celebration of it, we have sweet communion with Christ? In this gospel ordinance, Christ not only shows forth His beauty, but sends forth His virtue. The sacrament is not only a picture drawn, but a breast drawn. It gives us a taste of Christ as well as a sight (1 Peter 2:3). Such as make the sacrament only a representative of Christ shoot short of the mystery and come short of the comfort.

USE 2. It informs us of several things.

1. *It shows us the necessity of coming to the Lord's Supper.* Has Jesus Christ been at all this cost to make a feast?

Then, surely, there must be guests (Luke 22:19). It is not left to our choice whether we will come or not; it is a duty purely indispensable. "Let him eat of that bread" (1 Corinthians 11:28), which words are not only permissive, but authoritative. It is as if a king should say, "Let it be enacted."

The neglect of the sacrament runs men into a gospel penalty. It was infinite goodness in Christ to broach that blessed vessel of His body and let His sacred blood stream out. It is evil for us wilfully to omit such an ordinance wherein the trophy of mercy is so richly displayed and our salvation so nearly concerned. Well may Christ take this as an undervaluing of Him, and interpret it as no better than a bidding Him to keep His feast to Himself. He who did not observe the Passover was to be cut off (Numbers 9:13). How angry was Christ with those who stayed away from the supper! They thought to put it off with a compliment. But Christ knew how to construe their excuse for a refusal. "None of those men which were bidden shall taste of My supper" (Luke 14:24). Rejecting gospel mercy is a sin of so deep a die that God can do no less than punish it for a contempt. Some need a flaming sword to keep them from the Lord's Table, and others need Christ's whip of small cords to drive them to it.

Perhaps, some will say, they are above the sacrament. It would be strange to hear a man say that he is above his food! The apostles were not above this ordinance, and does anyone presume to be a peg higher than the apostles? Let all such consult that Scripture, "As often as ye eat this bread and drink this cup, ye show the Lord's death till He comes" (1 Corinthians 11:26). The Lord's death is to be remembered sacramentally till He comes to judgment.

2. *See the misery of unbelievers.* Though the Lord has appointed this glorious ordinance of His body and blood, they reap no benefit by it. They come to the sacrament either to keep up their credit or to stop the mouth of their conscience, but they get nothing for their souls. They come empty of grace and go away empty of comfort. "It shall even be as when a hungry man dreameth, and behold he eateth, but he awaketh, and his soul is empty" (Isaiah 29:8). So wicked men fancy that they eat of this spiritual banquet, but they are in a golden dream. Alas, they do not discern the Lord's body. The manna lay round about Israel's camp, but they did not know it. "They wist not what it was" (Exodus 16:15). So, carnal persons see the external elements, but Christ is not known to them in His saving virtues. There is honey in this spiritual rock which they never taste. They feed upon the bread, but not Christ in the bread. Isaac ate the kid when he thought it had been venison (Genesis 27:25). Unbelievers go away with the shadow of the sacrament. They have the rind and the husk, not the marrow. They eat the kid, not the venison.

3. *See in this text, as in a glass, infinite love displayed.*

(1) Behold the love of God the Father in giving Christ to be broken for us. That God should put such a jewel in pledge is the admiration of angels. "God so loved the world that He gave His only begotten Son" (John 3:16). It is a pattern of love without a parallel. It was a far greater expression of love in

God to give His Son to die for us than if He had voluntarily acquitted us of the debt without any satisfaction at all. If a subject is disloyal to his sovereign, it argues more love in the king to give his own son to die for that subject than to forgive him the wrong freely.

(2) That Christ should suffer death. "Lord," said Bernard, "Thou hast loved me more than Thyself; for Thou didst lay down Thy life for me." The emperor Trajan rent off a piece of his own robe to bind up one of his soldier's wounds. Christ rent off His own flesh for us. Nay, that Christ should die as the greatest sinner, having the weight of all men's sins laid upon Him, here was most transporting love! It sets all the angels in heaven wondering.

(3) That Christ should die freely. "I lay down My life" (John 10:17). There was no law to enjoin Him, no force to compel Him. It is called the "offering of the body of Jesus" (Hebrews 10:10). What could fasten Him to the cross but the golden link of love!

(4) That Christ should die for such as we are. What are we? Not only vanity, but enmity! When we were fighting, He was dying. When He had the weapons in our hands, then He had the spear in His side, Romans 5:8.

(5) That Christ died for us when He could not expect to be at all bettered by us. We were reduced to penury. We were in such a condition that we could neither merit Christ's love nor requite it. For Christ to die for us when we were at such a low ebb was the very quintessence of love. One man will extend kindness to another as long as he is able to requite him.

But if he is fallen to decay, then love begins to slacken and cool. But when we were engulfed in misery and fallen to decay, when we had lost our beauty, stained our blood, and spent our portion, then Christ died for us. O amazing love, which may swallow up all our thoughts!

(6) That Christ should not repent of His sufferings. "He shall see the travail of His soul and shall be satisfied" (Isaiah 53:11). It is a metaphor that alludes to a mother who, though she has suffered greatly, does not repent of it when she sees a child brought forth. So, though Christ had hard travail upon the cross, yet He does not repent of it, but thinks all His sufferings well-bestowed. He shall be satisfied. The Hebrew word signifies such a satiating as a man has at some sweet repast or banquet.

(7) That Christ should rather die for us than the angels that fell. They were creatures of a more noble extraction and, in all probability, might have brought greater revenues of glory to God. Yet, that Christ should pass by those golden vessels and make us clods of earth into stars of glory, O the hyperbole of Christ's love!

(8) Yet another step of Christ's love, for like the waters of the sanctuary it rises higher: that Christ's love should not cease at the hour of death! We write in our letters, "your friend till death." But Christ wrote in another style, "your Friend *after* death!" Christ died once, but loves forever. He is not testifying His affection to us. He is making the mansions ready for us (John 14:2). He is interceding for us (Hebrews 7:25). He appears in the court as the Advocate for the client. When He has finished dy-

ing, yet He has not finished loving. What a stupendous love was here! Who can meditate upon this and not be in ecstasy? Well may the Apostle call it "a love that passes knowledge" (Ephesians 3:19). When you see Christ broken in the sacrament, think of this love.

4. *See, then, what dear and entire affections we should bear to Christ, who gives us His body and blood in the eucharist.* If He had had anything to part with of more worth, He would have bestowed it upon us. O let Christ lie nearest our hearts! Let Him be our Tree of Life, and let us desire no other fruit. Let Him be our Morning Star, and let us rejoice in no other light.

As Christ's beauty, so His bounty should make Him loved by us. He has given us His blood as the price and His Spirit as the witness of our pardon. In the sacrament, Christ bestows all good things. He both imputes His righteousness and imparts His lovingkindness. He gives a foretaste of that supper which shall be celebrated in the paradise of God. To sum up all, in the blessed supper, Christ gives Himself to believers, and what can He give more? Dear Savior, how should Thy name be as ointment poured forth! The Persians worship the sun for their god. Let us worship the Sun of righteousness. Though Judas sold Christ for 30 pieces, let us rather part with all than this Pearl. Christ is that golden pipe through which the golden oil of salvation is transmitted to us.

Was Christ's body broken? Then we may behold sin odious in the red glass of Christ's sufferings. It is true, sin is to be abominated since it turned Adam out of paradise and threw the angels down to hell.

Sin is the peace-breaker. It is like an incendiary in the family that sets husband and wife at variance. It makes God fall out with us. Sin is the birthplace of our sorrows and the grave of our comforts. But that which may most of all disfigure the face of sin and make it appear abominable is this: It crucified our Lord! It made Christ veil His glory and lose His blood.

If a woman saw the sword that killed her husband, how hateful would the sight of it be to her! Do we count that sin light which made Christ's soul heavy unto death (Mark 14:34)? Can that be our joy which made the Lord Jesus a Man of sorrows (Isaiah 53:3)? Did He cry out, "My God, why hast Thou forsaken Me?" And shall not those sins be forsaken by us which made Christ Himself forsaken? O let us look upon sin with indignation! When a temptation comes to sin, let us say, as David, "Is not this the blood of the men that went in jeopardy of their lives?" (2 Samuel 23:17). So is not this the sin that poured out Christ's blood? Let our hearts be enraged against sin. When the senators of Rome showed the people Caesar's bloody robe, they were incensed against those that slew him. Sin has rent the white robe of Christ's flesh and died it a crimson color. Let us, then, seek to be avenged of our sins. Under the Law, if an ox gored a man so that he died, the ox was to be killed (Exodus 21:28). Sin has gored and pierced our Savior. Let it die the death. What a pity is it for that to live which would not suffer Christ to live!

Was Christ's body broken? Let us, then, from His suffering on the cross, learn this lesson not to wonder much if we meet with troubles in the world. Did Christ suffer who "knew no sin," and do we think it strange to suffer who know nothing *but* sin? Did Christ feel the anger of God? And is it much for us to feel the anger of men? Was the Head crowned with thorns? Must we have our bracelets and diamonds when Christ had the spear and nails going to His heart? Truly, such as are guilty may well expect the lash when He, who was innocent, could not go free.

USE 3. The third use is of exhortation, and it has several branches.

BRANCH 1. Was Christ's body broken for us? Let us be affected with the great goodness of Christ. Who can tread upon these hot coals and his heart not burn? Cry out with Ignatius, "Christ, my love, is crucified." If a friend should die for us, would not our hearts be much affected with his kindness? That the God of heaven should die for us, how should this stupendous mercy have a melting influence upon us! The body of Christ broken is enough to break the most flinty heart. At our Savior's passion, the very stones cleaved asunder. "The rocks rent" (Matthew 27:51). He who is not affected with this has a heart harder than the stones. If Saul was so affected with David's mercy in sparing his life (1 Samuel 24:16), how may we be affected with Christ's kindness who, to spare our life, lost His own! Let us pray that, as Christ was *crucifixus,* so He may be *cordi-fixus.* That is, as He was fastened to the cross, so He may be fastened to our hearts.

BRANCH 2. Is Jesus Christ spiritually exhibited to us in the sacrament? Let us then set a high value and estimate upon Him.

Let us prize Christ's body. Every crumb of this Bread of life is precious. "My flesh is meat indeed" (John 6:55). The manna was a lively type and emblem of Christ's body, for manna was sweet. "The taste of it was like wafers made with honey" (Exodus 16:31). It was a delicious food. Therefore it was called angel's food for its excellency. So Christ, the sacramental manna, is sweet to a believer's soul. "His fruit was sweet to my taste" (Song of Solomon 2:3). Everything of Christ is sweet. His name is sweet. His virtue is sweet. This manna sweetens the waters of Marah.

Nay, Christ's flesh excels manna. Manna was food, but not medicine. If an Israelite had been sick, manna could not have cured him. But this blessed manna of Christ's body is not only for food but for medicine. Christ has healing under His wings (Malachi 4:2). He heals the blind eye, the hard heart. Take this medicine next to your heart and it will heal you of all your spiritual distempers. Also, manna was corruptible. It ceased when Israel came to Canaan. But this blessed manna of Christ's body will never cease. The saints will feed with infinite delight and soul satisfaction upon Christ to all eternity. The joys of heaven would cease if this manna should cease. The manna was put in a golden pot in the ark to be preserved there. So the blessed manna of Christ's body, being put in the golden pot of the divine nature, is laid up in the ark of heaven for the support of saints forever. Well, then, may we say of Christ's blessed body, it is meat indeed. In the field of Christ's body, being digged upon the cross, we find the pearl of salvation.

Let us prize Christ's blood in the sacrament. It is drink indeed (John 6:55). Here is the nectar and ambrosia God Himself delights to taste of. This is both a balsam and a perfume.

Seven Supernatural Virtues in Christ's Blood

That we may set the higher value upon the blood of Christ, I shall show you seven rare supernatural virtues in it:

1. *It is a reconciling blood.* "You that were sometime alienated, and enemies, yet now hath He reconciled through death" (Colossians 1:21). Christ's blood is the blood of atonement. Nay, it is not only a sacrifice but a propitiation (1 John 2:2), which denotes a bringing us into favor with God. It is one thing for a traitor to be pardoned, and another thing to be brought into favor. Sin rent us off from God; Christ's blood cements us to God. If we had had as much grace as the angels, it could not have wrought our reconciliation. If we had offered up millions of holocausts and sacrifices, if we had wept rivers of tears, this could never have appeased an angry Deity. Only Christ's blood ingratiates us into God's favor and makes Him look upon us with a smiling aspect. When Christ died, the veil of the temple was rent. This was not without a mystery, to show that through Christ's blood the veil of our sins is rent which interposed between God and us.

2. *Christ's blood is a quickening blood.* "Whoso drinketh My blood, hath eternal life" (John 6:54). It both begets life and prevents death. "The life of a thing is

in the blood" (Leviticus 17:11). Sure enough, the life
of our soul is in the blood of Christ. When we contract deadness of heart, and are like wine that has
lost the spirits, Christ's blood has an elevating
power; it puts vivacity into us, making us quick and
lively in our motion. "They shall mount up with
wings as eagles" (Isaiah 40:31).

3. *Christ's blood is a cleansing blood.* "How much more
shall the blood of Christ purge your conscience!"
(Hebrews 9:14). As the merit of Christ's blood pacifies God, so the virtue of it purifies us. It is the king
of heaven's bath. It is a laver to wash in. It washes a
crimson sinner milk white. "The blood of Jesus
cleanseth us from all our sin" (1 John 1:7). The
Word of God is a looking glass to show us our spots,
and the blood of Christ is a fountain to wash them
away (Zechariah 13:1).

But this blood will not wash if it is mingled with
anything. If we go to mingle anything with Christ's
blood, either the merits of saints or the prayers of
angels, it will not wash. Let Christ's blood be pure
and unmixed, and there is no spot but it will wash
away. It purged out Noah's drunkenness and Lot's
incest. Indeed, there is one spot so black that
Christ's blood does not wash away, and that is the
sin against the Holy Ghost. Not but that there is
virtue enough in Christ's blood to wash it away, but
he who has sinned that sin will not be washed. He
condemns Christ's blood and tramples it under foot
(Hebrews 10:29).

4. *Christ's blood is a softening blood.* There is nothing
so hard but may be softened by this blood. It will
soften a stone. Water will soften the earth, but it will

not soften a stone; but Christ's blood mollifies a stone. It softens a heart of stone. It turns a flint into a spring. The heart, which before was like a piece hewn out of a rock, being steeped in Christ's blood, becomes soft and the waters of repentance flow from it. How was the jailer's heart dissolved and made tender when the blood of sprinkling was upon it! "Sirs, what must I do to be saved?" (Acts 16:30). His heart was now like melting wax. God might set what seal and impression He would upon it.

5. *Christ's blood cools the heart.* First, it cools the heart of sin. The heart naturally is full of distempered heat. It must be hot, being set on fire of hell. It burns in lust and passion. Christ's blood allays this heart and quenches the inflammation of sin. Second, it cools the heat of conscience. In times of desertion, conscience burns with the heat of God's displeasure. Now, Christ's blood, being sprinkled upon the conscience, cools and pacifies it. And, in this sense, Christ is compared to a river of water (Isaiah 32:2). When the heart burns and is in agony, Christ's blood is like water to the fire. It has a cooling, refreshing virtue in it.

6. *Christ's blood comforts the soul.* It is good against fainting fits. Christ's blood is better than wine. Though wine cheers the heart of a man who is well, yet it will not cheer his heart when he has a fit of the stone or when the pangs of death are upon him. But Christ's blood will cheer the heart at such a time. It is best in affliction. It cures the trembling of the heart.

A conscience sprinkled with Christ's blood can, like the nightingale, sing with a thorn at its breast.

The blood of Christ can make a prison become a
palace. It turned the martyr's flames into beds of
roses. Christ's blood gives comfort at the hour of
death. As a holy man once said on his deathbed
when they brought him a cordial, "No cordial like
the blood of Christ!"

7. *Christ's blood procures heaven.* Israel passed
through the Red Sea to Canaan. So, through the red
sea of Christ's blood, we enter into the heavenly
Canaan. "Having boldness therefore to enter into
the holiest by the blood of Jesus" (Hebrews 10:19).
Our sins shut heaven; Christ's blood is the key
which opens the gate of paradise for us. Hence it is
that Theodoret calls the cross the tree of salvation
because that blood which trickled down the cross
distils salvation. Well, then, may we prize the blood
of Christ and, with Paul, determine to know nothing
but Christ crucified (1 Corinthians 2:2). King's
crowns are only crosses, but the cross of Christ is the
only crown.

BRANCH 3. Does Christ offer His body and blood
to us in the Supper? Then with what solemn preparation should we come to so sacred an ordinance! It
is not enough to do *what* God has appointed, but *as*
He has appointed. "Prepare your hearts unto the
Lord" (1 Samuel 7:3). The musician first puts his instrument in tune before he plays. The heart must be
prepared and put in tune before it goes to meet with
God in this solemn ordinance of the sacrament.
Take heed of rashness and irreverence. If we do not
come prepared, we do not drink but spill Christ's
blood. "Whosoever shall eat this bread and drink
this cup of the Lord unworthily, shall be guilty of

the body and blood of the Lord" (1 Corinthians 11:27). "That is," said Theophylact, "he shall be judged a shedder of Christ's blood." We read of a wine cup of fury in God's hand (Jeremiah 25:15). He that comes unprepared to the Lord's Supper turns the cup in the sacrament into a cup of fury.

Oh, with what reverence and devotion should we address ourselves to these holy mysteries! The saints are called "prepared vessels" (Romans 9:23). If ever these vessels should be prepared, it is when they are to hold the precious body and blood of Christ. The sinner who is damned is first prepared. Men do not go to hell without some kind of preparation. "Vessels fitted for destruction" (Romans 9:22). If those vessels are prepared which are filled with wrath, much more are those to be prepared who are to receive Christ in the sacrament. Let us dress ourselves by a Scripture glass before we come to the Lord's Table and, with the Lamb's wife, make ourselves ready.

How Should We Prepare for the Lord's Supper?

1. *We must come with self-examining hearts.* "But let a man examine himself, and so let him eat of that bread" (1 Corinthians 11:28). It is not enough that others think we are fit to come, but we must examine ourselves. The Greek word "to examine" is a metaphor taken from the goldsmith who curiously tries his metals. So before we come to the Lord's Table, we are to make a curious and critical trial of ourselves by the Word.

Self-examination, being a reflexive act, is difficult. It is hard for a man to look inward and see the face of his own soul. The eye can see everything but itself.

But this work is necessary because, if we do not examine ourselves, we are at a loss about our spiritual estate. We know not whether we are interested in the covenant or whether we have a right to the seal. Also, because God will examine us. It was a sad question the master of the feast asked, "Friend, how camest thou in hither, not having a wedding garment?" (Matthew 22:12). So it will be terrible when God shall say to a man, "How did you come in here to My table with a proud, vain, unbelieving heart? What have you to do here in your sins. You pollute My holy things."

What need, therefore, is there to make a heart search before we come to the Lord's Supper! We should examine our sins that they may be mortified, our wants that they may be supplied, our graces that they may be strengthened.

2. *We must come with serious hearts.* Our spirits are feathery and light, like a vessel without ballast, which floats in the water but does not sail. We float in holy duties and are full of vain excursions, even when we are to deal with God and are engaged in matters of life and death. That which may consolidate our hearts and make them fix with seriousness is to consider that God's eye is now especially upon us when we approach His table. "The king came in to see the guests" (Matthew 22:11). God knows every communicant, and if He sees any levity and indecency of spirit in us, unworthy of His presence, He will be highly incensed and send us away with the

guilt of Christ's blood instead of the comfort of it.

3. *We must come with intelligent hearts.* There ought to be a competent measure of knowledge, that we may discern the Lord's body. As we are to pray with understanding (1 Corinthians 14:15), so ought we to communicate at the Lord's Table with understanding. If knowledge is lacking, it cannot be a reasonable service (Romans 12:1). They that do not know the mystery do not feel the comfort. We must know God the Father in His attributes, God the Son in His offices, God the Holy Ghost in His graces. Some say they have good hearts, yet lack knowledge. We may as well call that a good eye which lacks sight.

4. *We must come to the sacrament with longing hearts.* Say as Christ, "With desire I have desired to eat of this Passover" (Luke 22:15). If God prepares a feast, we must get an appetite. Why has the Lord frowned upon His people of late but to punish their surfeit and provoke their appetite? As David longed for the water of the well of Bethlehem (2 Samuel 23:15), so should we long for Christ in the sacrament. Desires are the sails of the soul which are spread to receive the gale of a heavenly blessing. For the exciting of holy desires and longings, consider:

(1) The magnificence and royalty of this supper. It is a heavenly banquet. "In this mountain shall the Lord of Hosts make unto all people a feast of fat things, a feast of wines on the lees" (Isaiah 25:6). Here is the juice of that grape which comes from the true Vine. Under these elements of bread and wine, Christ and all His benefits are exhibited to us. The sacrament is a repository and storehouse of celestial blessings. Behold here, life and peace and salvation

set before us! All the sweet delicacies of heaven are served in this feast.

(2) To provoke appetite, consider what need we have of this spiritual repast. The angel persuaded Elijah to take a little of the cake and jar of water that he might not faint in his journey. "Arise and eat, because the journey is too great for thee" (1 Kings 19:7). So truly we have a great journey from earth to heaven. Therefore, we need to recruit ourselves by the way. How many sins have we to subdue! How many duties to perform! How many wants to supply! How many graces to strengthen! How many adversaries to conflict with! So that we need refreshment by the way. By feeding upon the body and blood of the Lord, we renew our strength as the eagle.

(3) Consider Christ's readiness to dispense divine blessings in this ordinance. Jesus Christ is not a sealing fountain but a flowing fountain. It is but crying, and He gives us food. It is but thirsting, and He opens the conduit. "Let him that is athirst come; and whosoever will, let him take the water of life freely" (Revelation 22:17). As the clouds have natural proneness to drop down their moisture upon the earth, so has Christ to give forth of His gracious virtues and influences to the soul.

(4) There is no danger of excess at this supper. Other feasts often cause gluttony; it is not so here. The more we take of the Bread of life, the more healthful we are and the more we come to our spiritual complexion. Fullness here does not increase humours, but comforts. In spiritual things there is no extreme. Though a drop of Christ's blood is sweet, yet the more, the better—the deeper,

the sweeter. "Drink abundantly, O beloved," Song of Solomon 5:1.

(5) We do not know how long this feast may last. While the manna is to be had, let us bring our baskets. God will not always be spreading the cloth. If people lose their appetite, He will call to the enemy to take them away.

(6) Feeding upon Christ sacramentally will be a good preparation to sufferings. The Bread of life will help us to feed upon the bread of affliction. The cup of blessing will enable us to drink of the cup of persecution. Christ's blood is a wine that has a flavor in it and is full of spirits. Therefore, Cyprian tells us, when the primitive Christians were to appear before the cruel tyrants, they were wont to receive the sacrament, and then they arose up from the Lord's Table as lions breathing forth the fire of heavenly courage. Let these considerations be as sauce to sharpen our appetites to the Lord's Table. God loves to see us feed hungrily upon the Bread of life.

5. *If we would come prepared to this ordinance, we must come with penitent hearts.* The Passover was to be eaten with bitter herbs. We must bring our myrrh of repentance which, though it is bitter to us, is sweet to Christ. "They shall look upon Me whom they have pierced and mourn for Him" (Zechariah 12:10). A broken Christ is to be received with a broken heart. We that have sinned with Peter should weep with Peter. Our eyes should be filled with tears and our hearts steeped in the brinish waters of repentance. Say, "Lord Jesus, though I cannot bring sweet spices, and perfume Thy body as Mary did, yet I will wash Thy feet with my tears." The more bitterness we taste

in sin, the more sweetness we shall taste in Christ.

6. *We must come with sincere hearts.* The tribes of Israel, being straitened in time, wanted some legal purifications. Yet because their hearts were sincere and they came with desire to meet with God in the Passover, therefore the Lord healed the people (2 Chronicles 30:19–20). Bad aims will spoil good actions. An archer may miss the mark as well by squinting as by shooting short. What is our design in coming to the sacrament? Is it that we may have more victory over our corruptions and be more confirmed in holiness? Then God will be good to us and heal us. Sincerity, like true gold, shall have some grains allowed for its lightness.

7. *We must come with hearts fired with love to Christ.* The spouse said, "I am sick of love" (Song of Solomon 2:5). Let us give Christ the wine of our love to drink and weep that we can love Him no more. Would we have Christ's exhilarating presence in the Supper? Let us meet Him with strong endearments of affection. Basil compares love to a sweet ointment. Christ delights to smell this perfume. The disciple that loved most, Christ put in His bosom.

8. *We must come with humble hearts.* We see Christ humbling Himself to death. And will a humble Christ ever be received into a proud heart? A sight of God's glory and a sight of sin may humble us. Was Christ humble, who was all purity? And are we proud, who are all leprosy? O let us come with a sense of our own vileness. How humble should he be who is to receive alms of free grace? Jesus Christ is a lily of the valley (Song of Solomon 2:1), not of the mountains. Humility was never a loser. The

emptier the vessel is, and the lower it is let down into the well, the more water it draws up. So the more the soul is emptied of itself, and the lower it is let down by humility, the more it fetches out of the well of salvation. God will come into a humble heart to revive it (Isaiah 57:15). That is none of Christ's temple which is not built with a low roof.

9. *We must come with heavenly hearts.* The mystery of the sacrament is heavenly. What should an earthworm do here? He is not likely to feed on Christ's body and blood who, with the serpent, eats dust. The sacrament is called "communion" (1 Corinthians 10:16). What communion can earthly man have with Christ? First, there must be conformity before communion. He that is earthly is no more conformed in likeness to Christ than a clod of dust is like a star. An earthly man makes the world his god. Then let him not think to receive another God in the sacrament. O let us be in the heavenly altitudes and, by the wing of grace, ascend!

10. *We must come with believing hearts.* Christ gave the sacrament to the apostles, principally as they were believers. Such as come faithless go away fruitless. Nor it is enough to have the habit of faith. We must exert and put forth the vigorous actings of faith in this ordinance.

(1) Let us exercise the eye of faith. Faith has an eagle's eye. It pierces into things far remote from sense. Faith takes a prospect of heaven. It discerns Him who is invisible (Hebrews 11:27). It beholds a beauty and fulness in Christ. It sees this beauty shining through the lattice of an ordinance. Faith views Christ's love streaming in His blood. Look upon

Christ with believing eyes and you shall, one day, see Him with glorified eyes.

(2) Exercise the mouth of faith. Here is the bread broken. What use is there of bread but to feed on? Feed upon the Bread of God. Adam died by eating; we live by eating. In the sacrament, the whole Christ is presented to us, the divine and the human nature. All kind of virtue comes from Him, mortifying, mollifying, comforting. Oh, then, feed on Him! This grace of faith is the great grace to be set on work at the sacrament.

QUESTION. Does the virtue lie simply in faith?

ANSWER. Not in faith considered purely as a grace, but as it has respect to the object. The virtue is not in faith, but in Christ. Consider this: a ring which has a precious stone in it which will staunch blood. We say that the ring staunches blood, but it is the stone in the ring. So faith is the ring, Christ is the precious stone. All that faith does is to bring home Christ's merits to the soul, and so it justifies. The virtue is not in faith but in Christ.

QUESTION. But why should faith carry away more from Christ in the sacrament than any other grace?

ANSWER 1. Because faith is the most receptive grace. It is the receiving of gold which enriches. So faith, receiving Christ's merits and filling the soul with all the fulness of God, must be an enriching grace. In the body, there are veins that suck the nourishment which comes into the stomach and turns it into blood and spirits. Faith is such a sucking vein that draws virtue from Christ. Therefore it is called a precious faith (2 Peter 1:1).

ANSWER 2. Faith has more of Christ's benefits annexed to it because it is the most humble grace. If repentance should fetch justification from Christ, a man would be ready to say, "This was for my tears." But faith is humble; it is an empty hand, and what merit can there be in that? Does a poor man, reaching out his hand, merit an alms? So because faith is humble, and gives all the glory to Christ and free grace, hence it is that God has put so much honor on it. This shall be the grace to which Christ and all His merits belong. Therefore, above all graces, set faith to work in the sacrament. Faith fetches in all provisions. This is the golden bucket that draws water out of the well of life.

But there is a bastard faith in the world. Pliny tells of a Cyprian stone which is, in color and splendor, like the diamond, but it is not of the right kind. It will break with the hammer. So, there is a false faith which sparkles and makes a show in the eye of the world, but it is not genuine; it will break with the hammer of persecution.

Six Differences Between a Sincere Faith and a Hypocritical Faith

Therefore, to prevent mistakes, and that we may not be deceived and think we believe when we only presume, I shall give you six differences between a sincere faith, which is the flower of the spirit, and a hypocritical faith, which is the fruit of fancy.

1. *A hypocritical faith is easy to come by.* It is like the seed in the parable which sprung up suddenly

(Mark 4:5). A false faith shoots up without any convictions and soul humblings. As Isaac said, "How comest thou by thy venison so soon?" (Genesis 27:20). Likewise, how does this man come by faith so soon? Surely it is of different nature and will quickly wither away. But true faith, being an an outlandish plant and of a heavenly extraction, is hard to come by. It costs many a sigh and tear (Acts 2:37). This spiritual infant is not born without pangs.

2. *A hypocritical faith is afraid to come to trial.* The hypocrite would rather have his faith commended than examined. He can no more endure a Scripture trial than counterfeit metal can endure the touchstone. He is like a man who has stolen goods in his house and is very unwilling to have his house searched. So the hypocrite has gotten some stolen goods that the devil has helped him to, and he is loathe to have his heart searched. Whereas true faith is willing to come to a trial. "Examine me, O Lord, and prove me; try my reins and heart" (Psalm 26:2). David was not afraid to be tried by a jury, no, though God Himself was one of the jury. Good wares are never afraid of the light.

3. *A hypocritical faith has a slight esteem of true faith.* The hypocrite hears others speak in the commendation of faith, but he wonders where the virtue of it lies. He looks upon faith as a drug, or some base commodity that will not go off. He will part with all the faith he has for a piece of silver and, perhaps, it might be dear enough at the price. But the man who has true faith sets a high value on it. He reckons this grace among his jewels. What incorporates him into Christ but faith? What puts him into a state of son-

ship but faith (Galatians 3:26)? O precious faith! A believer would not exchange his shield of faith for a crown of gold!

4. *A hypocritical faith is lame on one hand.* With one hand it would take up Christ. But it does not with the other hand give itself up to Christ. It would take Christ by way of surety, but not give up itself to Him by way of surrender. True faith, however, is impartial. It takes Christ as a Savior and submits to Him as a Prince. Christ said, "With My body and My blood, I endow thee." And faith says, "With my soul, I worship Thee."

5. *A hypocritical faith is impure.* The hypocrite says he believes, yet goes on in sin. He is all creed, but no commandment. He believes, yet will take God's name in vain. "Wilt thou not cry unto me, 'My Father, Thou art the guide of my youth!' Behold, Thou hast done evil things as thou couldst" (Jeremiah 3:4–5). These impostors would call God their Father, yet sin as fast as they could. For one to say he has faith, yet live in sin, is as if a man should say he was in health, yet his vitals had perished. But a true faith is joined with sanctity. "Holding the mystery of faith in a pure conscience" (1 Timothy 3:9). The jewel of faith is always put in the cabinet of a good conscience. The woman who touched Christ by faith felt a healing virtue come from Him. Though faith does not wholly remove sin, yet it subdues it.

6. *A hypocritical faith is a dead faith; it tastes no sap or sweetness in Christ.* The hypocrite tastes something in the vine and olive. He finds contentment in the carnal, luscious delights of the world, but no sweetness

in a promise. The Holy Ghost Himself is spiritless to him. That is a dead faith which has no sense or taste. But true faith finds much delight in heavenly things. The Word is sweeter than the honeycomb (Psalm 19:10). Christ's love is better than wine (Song of Solomon 1:2). Thus we see a difference between true and spurious faith. How many have thought they have had the live child of faith by them, when it has proved the dead child. Take heed of presumption, but cherish faith. Faith applies Christ and makes a spiritual concoction of His body and blood. This supper was intended chiefly for believers (Luke 22:19). Christ's blood to an unbeliever is like *aquavitae* in a dead man's mouth: it loses all its virtue.

11.* *We must come to the Lord's Table with charitable hearts.* "Purge out, therefore, the old leaven" (1 Corinthians 5:7). The leaven of malice will sour the ordinance to us. We must come with bitter tears, yet not with bitter spirits. The Lord's Supper is a love feast. Christ's blood was shed not only to reconcile us to God but to one another. Christ's body was broken to make up the breaches among Christians. How sad is it that they who profess they are going to eat Christ's flesh in the sacrament should tear the flesh of one another! "Whosoever hateth his brother is a murderer" (1 John 3:15). He who comes to the Lord's Table in hatred is a Judas to Christ and a Cain to his brother. What benefit can he receive at the sacrament whose heart is poisoned with malice?

If one drinks poison and immediately takes

---

* This point follows point 10 from page 158.

medicine, surely the medicine will do him no good. Such as are poisoned with rancour and malice are not the better for the sacramental medicine. He that does not come in charity to the sacrament has nothing of God in him, for "God is love" (1 John 4:16). He knows nothing of the gospel savingly, for it is a gospel of peace (Ephesians 6:15). He has none of the wisdom which comes from heaven, for that is gentle and easy to be entreated (James 3:17). Oh, that Christians were rooted and cemented together in love! Shall devils unite and saints divide? Did we thus learn Christ? Has not the Lord Jesus loved us to the death? What greater reproach can be cast upon such a loving Head than for the members to smite one against another? The good Lord put out the fire of contention and kindles the fire of love and amity in all our hearts.

12. *We must come with praying hearts.* Every ordinance, as well as every creature, is sanctified by prayer (1 Timothy 4:5). Prayer turns the element into spiritual aliment. When we send the dove of prayer to heaven, it brings an olive leaf in its mouth. We should pray that God would enrich His ordinance with His presence; that He would make the sacrament effectual to all those holy ends and purposes for which He has appointed it; that it may be the feast of our graces and the funeral of our corruptions; that it may be not only a sign to represent, but an instrument to convey Christ to us, and a seal to assure us of our heavenly union. If we would have the fat and sweet of this ordinance, we must send prayer before, as a harbinger, to bespeak a blessing.

Some are so distracted with worldly cares that

they can scarcely spare any time for prayer before they come to the sacrament. Do they think the tree of blessing will drop its fruit into their mouth when they never shook it by prayer? God does not set His mercies at so low a rate as to cast them away upon those who do not seek them (Ezekiel 36:37).

Nor is it enough to pray, but it must be with heat and intensity of soul. Jacob wrestled in prayer (Genesis 32:24). Cold prayers, like cold suitors, never speed. Prayer must be with sighs and groans (Romans 8:26). It must be in the Holy Ghost (Jude 20). "He who will speak to God," said St. Ambrose, "must speak to Him in His own language which He understands," that is, in the language of His Spirit.

13. *We must come to the Lord's Table with self-denying hearts.* When we have prepared ourselves in the best manner we can, let us take heed of trusting our preparations. "When ye shall have done all these things which are commanded you, say, 'We are unprofitable servants' " (Luke 17:10). Use duty, but do not idolize it. We ought to use duties to fit us for Christ, but we must not make a Christ of our duties. Duty is the golden path to walk in, but not a silver crutch to lean on. Alas! What are all our preparations? God can spy a hole in our best garments. "All our righteousness is as filthy rags" (Isaiah 64:6). When we have prepared ourselves as hoping in God's mercy, we must deny ourselves as deserving His justice. If our holiest services are not sprinkled with Christ's blood, they are no better than shining sins and, like Uriah's letter, they carry in them the matter of our death. Use duty, but trust Christ and free grace for acceptance. Be like Noah's dove: she

made use of her wings to fly, but trusted in the ark for safety.

We see how we are to be qualified in our addresses to the Lord's Table. Thus coming, we shall meet with embraces of mercy. We shall have not only a representation but a participation of Christ in the sacrament. We shall be filled with all the fulness of God (Ephesians 3:19).

BRANCH 4.* Has Jesus Christ made this gospel banquet? Is He both the Founder and the Feast? Then let poor, doubting Christians be encouraged to come to the Lord's Table. Satan would hinder from the sacrament, as Saul hindered the people from eating honey (1 Samuel 14:26). But is there any soul that has been humbled and bruised for sin, whose heart secretly pants after Christ, but yet stands trembling and dares not approach to these holy mysteries? Let me encourage that soul to come. "Arise, He calleth thee" (Mark 10:49).

OBJECTION 1. But I am sinful and unworthy, and why should I meddle with such holy things?

ANSWER. Who did Christ die for but such? "He came into the world to save sinners" (1 Timothy 1:15). He took our sins upon Him as well as our nature. "He bore our griefs" (Isaiah 53:4). In the Hebrew it is "our sicknesses." "See your sins," said Luther, "upon Christ, and then they are no more yours but His." Our sins should humble us, but they must not discourage us from coming to Christ. The more diseased we are, the rather we should step into

---

* Branch 4 follows Branch 3 from page 151.

this pool of Siloam. Who does Christ invite to the supper but the poor, halted, and maimed? (Luke 14:21)—that is, such as see themselves unworthy and fly to Christ for sanctuary. The priest was to take a bunch of hyssop, dip it in blood, and sprinkle it upon the leper (Leviticus 14:6–7). You who have the leprosy of sin upon you, yet if, as a leper, you loathe yourself, Christ's precious blood shall be sprinkled upon you.

OBJECTION 2. But I have sinned presumptuously against mercy. I have contracted guilt after I have been at the Lord's Table, and surely Christ's blood is not for me.

ANSWER. It is, indeed, grievous to abuse mercy. It was the aggravation of Solomon's sin. His heart was turned from the Lord "who had appeared to him twice" (1 Kings 11:9). Presumptuous sins open the mouth of conscience to accuse and shut the mouth of God's Spirit, which should speak peace. Yet do not cast away your anchor. Look up to the blood of Christ. It can forgive sins against mercy. Did not Noah sin against mercy, who, though he had been so miraculously preserved in the flood, yet soon after he came out of the ark was drunk? Did not David sin against mercy when, after God had made him king, he stained his soul with lust and his robe with blood? Yet both these sins were washed away in that fountain which is set open for Judah to wash in (Zechariah 13:1).

Did not the disciples deal unkindly with Christ in the time of His suffering? Peter denied Him, and all the rest fled from His colors. "Then all the disciples forsook Him and fled" (Matthew 26:56). Yet

Christ did not take advantage of their weakness, nor did He cast them off, but sends the joyful news of His resurrection to them (Matthew 27:63), and of His ascension. "Go to my brethren and say unto them, 'I ascend to My Father, and your Father' " (John 20:17). And, lest Peter should think he was none of the number that should be interested in Christ's love, therefore Christ dispatched away a special message to Peter to comfort him. "Go tell the disciples and Peter, that He goes before you into Galilee, there shall ye see Him" (Mark 16:7). So that where our hearts are sincere and our turnings aside are rather from a defect in our power than our will, the Lord Jesus will not take advantage of every failing. Instead He will drop His blood upon us, which has a voice in it which speaks better things than the blood of Abel (Hebrews 12:24).

OBJECTION 3. But I find such a faintness and feebleness in my soul that I dare not go to the Lord's Table.

ANSWER. You have all the more need to go. Drink of this wine for your infirmities (1 Timothy 5:23). Would it not be strange for a man to argue thus: "My body is weak and declining; therefore, I will not go to the physician." He should the rather go! Our weakness should send us to Christ. His blood is mortal to sin and vital to grace. You say you have defects in your soul. If you had none, there would be no need of a Mediator, nor would Christ have any work to do. Oh, therefore, turn your disputing into believing. Be encouraged to come to this blessed Supper. You shall find Christ giving forth His sweet influences and your grace shall flourish as an herb.

OBJECTION 4. But I have often come to this ordinance and found no fruit. I am not filled with comfort.

ANSWER. God may meet you in an ordinance when you do not discern it. Christ was with Mary, yet she did not know it was Christ. You think Christ has not met you at His table because He does not give you comfort.

Though He does not fill you with comfort, He may fill you with strength. We think we have no answer from God in a duty unless He fills us with joy. Yet God may manifest His presence as well by giving strength as comfort. If we have power from heaven to foil our corruptions and to walk more closely and evenly with God, this is an answer from God. "I will strengthen them in the Lord" (Zechariah 10:12). If, Christian, you do not have God's arm to embrace you, yet if you have His arm to strengthen you, this is the fruit of an ordinance.

If God does not fill your heart with joy, yet if He fills your eyes with tears, this is His meeting you at His table. When you look upon Christ broken on the cross, and consider His love and your ingratitude, this makes the dew begin to fall, and your eyes are like the fish pools in Heshbon, full of water (Song of Solomon 7:4). This is God's graciously meeting with you in the sacrament. Bless His name for it. It is a sign the Sun of righteousness has risen upon us, when our frozen hearts melt in tears for sin.

If your comforts are low, yet if the actings of your faith are high, this is God's manifesting His presence in the Supper. The sensible tokens of God's love are withheld, but the soul ventures on Christ's blood. It believes that, coming to Him, He will hold out the golden sceptre (John 6:37). This glorious acting of faith, and the inward quiet that faith breeds, is the blessed return of an ordinance. "He will turn again, He will have compassion on us" (Micah 7:19). The church's comforts were darkened, but her faith breaks forth as the sun out of a cloud. He will have compassion on us. This acting of faith makes us in a blessed condition. "Blessed are they which have not seen, yet have believed" (John 20:29).

OBJECTION 5. But I cannot find any of these things in the sacrament. My heart is dead and locked up and I have no return at all.

ANSWER. Wait on God for an answer of the ordinance. God has promised to fill the soul. "He filleth the hungry soul with goodness" (Psalm 107:9). If not with gladness, yet with goodness. The soul must be filled or how can the promise be fulfilled? Christian! God has said it. Therefore wait. Will you not believe God unless you have a voice from heaven? The Lord has given you His promise. And is it not as good security to have a bill under a man's hand as to have it by word of mouth? Be content to wait awhile, mercy will come. God's mercies in Scripture are not called speedy mercies, but they are called sure mercies (Isaiah 55:3).

BRANCH 5. Has Christ given us His body's blood? Then when we are at this gospel ordinance, let us remember the Lord Jesus there. The sacrament is a Christ-remembering ordinance. "This do in remembrance of Me" (1 Corinthians 11:25). God has appointed this spiritual festival to preserve the living memory of our dying Savior. A sacrament-day is a commemoration day.

Remember Christ's passion. "Remembering the wormwood and the gall" (Lamentations 3:19). I may alter the words a little: "Remembering the vinegar and the gall." If the manna was to be kept in the ark so that the memory of it should be preserved, how should the death and suffering of Christ be kept in our minds as a memorial when we are at the Table of the Lord?

Remember the glorious benefits we receive from the broken body of Christ. We usually remember those things which are advantageous to us. Christ's broken body is a screen to keep off the fire of God's wrath from us. Christ's body being broken, the serpent's head is broken. Christ being broken upon the cross, a box of precious jewels is broken open. Now we have access to God with boldness. The blood of the cross has made way to the throne of grace. Now we are made sons and heirs, and to be heir to the promise is better than to be heir to the crown. Christ having died, we are made near akin to the blessed Trinity. We are candidates and expectants of glory. The bloody way of the cross is our milky way to heaven. Jesus Christ drank gall that we might drink the honey streams of Canaan. His cross was stuck full of nails that our crown might be hung full of jewels. Well may we remember Christ in the blessed sacrament!

But the bare remembrance of Christ's death is not enough. Some who have a natural tenderness of spirit may be affected with the history of Christ's passion, but this remembrance of Christ has little comfort in it. Let us remember Christ in the sacrament rightly.

Let us remember Christ's death with joy. "God forbid that I should glory, save in the cross of our Lord Jesus Christ" (Galatians 6:14). When we see Christ in the sacrament crucified before our eyes, we may behold Him in that posture as He was in upon the cross, stretching out His blessed arms to receive us. O what matter of triumph and acclamation is this! Though we remember our sins with grief, yet we should remember Christ's sufferings with joy. Let us weep for those sins which shed His blood, yet rejoice in that blood which washes away our sins.

Let us so remember Christ's death as to be conformed to His death. "That I may be conformable to His death" (Philippians 3:10). Then we remember Christ's death rightly when we are dead with Him. Our pride and passion are dead. Christ's dying for us makes sin die in us. Then we rightly remember Christ's crucifixion when we are crucified with Him. We are dead to the pleasures and preferments of the world. "The world is crucified unto me, and I to the world" (Galatians 6:14).

BRANCH 6. If Christ has given us this soul festival for the strengthening of grace, let us labor to feel some virtue flowing out of this ordinance to us. It would be strange if a man should receive no nourishment from his food. It is a discredit to this ordinance if we get no increase of grace. Shall leanness enter into our souls at a feast of fat things? Christ gives us His body and blood for the augmenting of faith. He expects that we should reap some profit and income, and that our weak, minute faith should flourish into a great faith. "O woman, great is thy faith" (Matthew 15:28). It would be good to examine whether, after our frequent celebration of this holy Supper, we have arrived at a great faith.

QUESTION. How may I know whether I have this great faith?

ANSWER. For the solution of this, I shall lay down six eminent signs of a great faith. And, if we can show any one of them, we have made a good proficiency at the sacrament.

Six Signs of a Great Faith

1. *A great faith can trust God without a pledge.* It can rely upon providence in the deficiency of outward supplies. "Although the fig tree shall not blossom, neither shall fruit be in the vines, the labor of the olive shall fail, yet will I rejoice in the Lord" (Habakkuk 3:17–18). An unbeliever must have something to feed his senses or he gives up the ghost. When he is at his wealth's end, he is at his wit's end. Faith does not question but that God will provide, though it does not see which way provisions should come in. Faith does not fear famine. God has set His seal to it, "Verily thou shalt be fed" (Psalm 37:3). Faith puts the bond in suit. "Lord," says faith, "wilt Thou feed the birds of the air, and wilt not Thou feed me? Shall I lack when my Father keeps the purse?" A good Christian with the rod of faith smites the Rock in heaven, and some honey and oil comes out for recruiting his present necessities.

2. *A great faith is a wonder-working faith.* It can do

those things which exceed the power of nature. A great faith can open heaven. It can overcome the world (1 John 5:4). It can master an easily-besetting sin (2 Samuel 22:24). It can prefer the glory of God before secular interest (Romans 9:1). It can rejoice in affliction (1 Thessalonians 1:6). It can bridle the intemperance of passion; it can shine forth in the hemisphere of its relations; it can do duties in a more refined, sublimated manner, mixing love with duty, which mellows it and makes it taste more pleasant. It can antedate glory and make things at the greatest distance to unite. Thus the springhead of faith rises higher than nature. A man, by the power of nature, can no more do this than iron can of itself swim or the earth ascend.

3. *A great faith is firm and steadfast; weak faith is frequently shaken with fears and doubt.* A great faith is like an oak that spreads its roots deep and is not easily blown down (Colossians 2:7). A great faith is like the anchor or cable of a ship that holds it steady in the midst of storms. A Christian who is steeled with this heroic faith is settled in the mysteries of religion. The Spirit of God has so firmly printed heavenly truths upon his heart that you may as well remove the sun out of the firmament as remove him from those holy principles he has imbibed. Behold here a pillar in the temple of God (Revelation 3:12).

4. *A great faith can trust in an angry God; it believes God's love through a frown.* A vigorous faith, though it is repulsed and beaten back, yet will come on again and press upon God with a holy obstinacy. The woman of Canaan was three times repulsed by Christ, yet she would take no denial from Him. She

turned discouragements into arguments and made a fresh onset upon Christ until at last, by the power of faith, she overcame Him. "O woman, great is thy faith; be it unto thee even as thou wilt" (Matthew 15:28). The key of her faith unlocked Christ's heart, and now she may have what she will from Him. When once she had gotten His heart, she might have His treasure too.

5. *A great faith can swim against the tide.* It can go cross to sense and reason. Corrupt faith says, as Peter, "Master, pity Thyself." Faith says, "It is better to suffer than to sin." Reason consults safety; faith will hazard safety to preserve sanctity. A believer can sail to heaven, though the tide of reason and the wind of temptation are against him.

Abraham, in the case of sacrificing his son, did not call reason to the council board. When God said, "Offer up your son, Isaac," it was enough to pose not only fleshly wisdom, but even faith too. For here, the commands of God seemed to interfere. In one command, the Lord said, "Thou shalt not murder," and, behold, here a quite contrary command, "Offer up thy son." So that Abraham in obeying one command seemed to disobey another. Besides, Isaac was a son of the promise. The Messiah was to come of Isaac's line (Hebrews 11:18). And if he was cast off, how would the world have a Mediator? Here was enough to puzzle this holy patriarch. Yet, Abraham's faith unties all these knots and the bloody knife is made ready.

Abraham believed that when God called for it, it was not murder but sacrifice, and that the Lord, having made a promise of Christ's springing up out of

Isaac's loins, rather than the promise should fall to the ground, God could raise up seed out of Isaac's ashes. Here was a giant faith, which God Himself set a trophy of honor upon. "By Myself I have sworn, saith the Lord, for because thou hast done this thing, and hast not withheld thy son, thine only son, that in blessing I will bless thee" (Genesis 22:16).

6. *A great faith can bear great delays.* Though God does not give an immediate answer to prayer, faith believes it shall have an answer in due time. A weak faith is soon out of breath and, if it does not have the mercy immediately, it begins to faint. Whereas he who has a strong, powerful faith does not make haste (Isaiah 28:16). A great faith is content to stay God's leisure. Faith will trade with God for time.

"Lord," says faith, "if I do not have the mercy I want instantly, I will trust longer. I know my money is in good hands. An answer of peace will come. Perhaps the mercy is not yet ripe or, perhaps, I am not ripe for the mercy. Lord, do as it seems good in Thine eyes."

Faith knows the most tedious voyages have the richest returns, and, the longer mercy is in expectation, the sweeter it will be in fruition. Behold here a glorious faith. If we have such a faith as this to show, it is a blessed fruit of our sacramental converse with God.

But I would not discourage infant believers. If your grace is not risen to the bigness and proportion of a great faith, but is of the proper kind, it shall find acceptance. God, who bids us receive Him who is weak in faith (Romans 14:1), will not Himself refuse him. If your faith is not grown to a cedar, yet is a bruised reed, it is too good to be broken (Matthew 12:20). A weak faith can lay hold on a strong Christ. A palsied hand may tie the knot in marriage.

Only do not let Christians rest in lower measures of grace, but aspire after higher degrees. The stronger our faith, the firmer our union with Christ and the more sweet influence we draw from Him. This is that which honors the blessed sacrament, when we can show the increase of grace and, being strong in faith, bring glory to God (Romans 4:20).

BRANCH 7. Has Christ provided such a blessed banquet for us? He does not nurse us abroad, but feeds us with His own breast, nay, His own blood. Let us, then, study to answer this great love of Christ. It is true, we can never parallel His love. Yet let us show ourselves thankful. We can do nothing satisfactory, but we may do something gratulatory. Christ gave Himself as a sin offering for us. Let us give ourselves as a thank offering for Him. If a man redeems another out of debt, will he not be grateful? How deeply do we stand obliged to Christ, who has redeemed us from hell!

Let us show thankfulness four ways:

1. *By courage.* Christ has set us a copy. He did not fear men, but endured the cross and despised the shame. Let us be steeled with courage, being made ready to suffer for Christ, which is, as Chrysostom said, to be baptized with a baptism of blood. Did Christ bear the wrath of God for us, and shall we not bear the wrath of men for Him? It is our glory to suffer in Christ's quarrel. "The Spirit of God and of

glory resteth upon you" (1 Peter 4:14). Let us pray for
furnace grace. Be like those three children. "Be it
known to thee, O king, that we will not serve thy
gods" (Daniel 3:18). They would rather burn than
bow. Oh, that such a spirit as was in Cyprian might
survive in us! The proconsul would have tempted
him for his religion and said to him, "Consult for
your safety." Cyprian responded, "In so just a cause,
there needs no consultation." When the sentence of
his death was read, he replied, "Thanks be to God."

We do not know how soon an hour of temptation
may come. Oh, remember, Christ's body was broken! His blood poured out. We have no such blood
to shed for Him as He shed for us.

2. *Let us show our thankfulness to Christ by fruitfulness.*
Let us bring forth the sweet fruits of patience, heav-
enly-mindedness, and good works. This is to live
unto Him who died for us (2 Corinthians 5:15). If we
would rejoice the heart of Christ, and make Him not
to repent of His sufferings, let us be fertile in obedience. The wise men not only worshiped Christ, but
presented unto Him gifts, gold and frankincense
(Matthew 2:11). Let us present Christ with the best
fruits of our garden. Let us give Him our love, that
flower of delight. The saints are not only compared
to stars for their knowledge, but spice trees for their
fertileness. The breasts of the spouse were like clus-
ters of grapes (Song of Solomon 7:7). The blood of
Christ received in a spiritual manner is like the water of jealousy, which had a virtue both to kill and to
make fruitful (Numbers 5:27–28). Christ's blood
kills sin and makes the hearts fructify in grace.

3. *Let us show our thankfulness to Christ by our zeal.*

How zealous was Christ for our redemption! Zeal turns a saint into a seraphim. A true Christian has a double baptism, one of water, the other of fire. He is baptized with the fire of zeal. Be zealous for Christ's name and worship. Zeal is increased by opposition. It cuts its way through the rocks. Zeal loves truth most when it is disgraced and hated. "They have made void Thy law; therefore I love Thy commandments above gold" (Psalm 119:126–127).

How little thankfulness do they show to Christ who have no zeal for His honor and interest! They are like Ephraim. "Ephraim is a cake not turned" (Hosea 7:8), baked on one side and dough on the other. Christ most abominates a lukewarm temper (Revelation 3:15). He is even sick of such professors. Those who write of the situation of England say that it is seated between the torrid and frigid zone. The climate is neither very hot nor cold. I wish this were not the temper of the people and that our hearts were not too like the climate we live in. May the Lord cause the fire of holy zeal to always be burning upon the altar of our hearts.

4. *Let us show our thankfulness by universal subjection to Christ.* This is to make the Lord's Supper, in a spiritual sense, a feast of dedication, when we renew our vows and give ourselves up to God's service. "Truly I am Thy servant, I am Thy servant" (Psalm 116:16). "Lord, all I have is Thine. My head shall be Thine to study for Thee; my hands shall be Thine to work for Thee; my heart shall be Thine to adore Thee; my tongue shall be Thine to praise Thee."

BRANCH 8. If Jesus Christ has provided so holy an ordinance as the sacrament, let us walk suitably to it. Have we received Christ into our hearts? Let us show Him forth by our heavenliness.

Let us show forth Christ by our heavenly words. Let us speak the language of Canaan. When the Holy Ghost came upon the apostles, they spoke with other tongues (Acts 2:4). While we speak the words of grace and soberness, our lips smell like perfume and drip like honey.

Let us show forth Christ by our heavenly affections. Let our sighs and breathings after God go up as a cloud of incense. "Set your affections on things above" (Colossians 3:2). We should do by our affections as the husbandmen do by their corn. If the corn lies low in a damp room, it is in danger of corruption. Therefore, they carry it up into their highest room that it may keep the better. So our affections, if set on earth, are apt to corrupt and be unsavory. Therefore, we should carry them up on high above the world that they may be preserved pure. Breathe after fuller revelations of God. Desire to attain unto the resurrection of the dead (Philippians 3:11). The higher our affections are raised towards heaven, the sweeter joys we feel. The higher the lark flies, the sweeter it sings.

Let us show forth Christ by our heavenly conversation (Philippians 3:20). Hypocrites may, in a pang of conscience, have some good affections stirred, but they are as flushes of heat in the face which come and go. But the constant tenor of our life must be holy. We must shine forth in a kind of angelic sanctity. As it is with a piece of coin, it does not have only the king's image within a ring but his superscription without. So it is not enough to have the image of Christ in the heart, but there must be the superscription without. Something of Christ must be written in the life.

The scandalous lives of many communicants are a reproach to the sacrament and tempt others to infidelity. How odious it is that those hands which have received the sacramental elements should take bribes! That those eyes which have been filled with tears at the Lord's Table should, afterwards, be filled with envy! That those teeth, which have eaten holy bread, should grind the faces of the poor! That those lips, which have touched the sacramental cup, should salute a harlot! That the mouth which has drunk consecrated wine should be full of oaths! That they who seem to deify Christ in the eucharist should vilify Him in His members! In a word, that such as pretend to eat Christ's body and drink His blood at church should eat the bread of wickedness and drink the wine of violence in their own houses (Proverbs 4:17). These are like those Italians I have read of who, at the sacrament, are so devout, as if they believed God to be in the bread, but in their lives are so profane, as if they did not believe God to be in heaven. Such as these are apt to make the world think that the gospel is but a fancy or a religious cheat. What shall I say of them? With Judas, they receive the devil in the sop, and are no better than crucifiers of the Lord of glory. As their sin is heinous, so their punishment will be proportionable. "They eat and drink damnation to themselves" (1 Corinthians 11:29).

Oh, that such a luster and majesty of holiness sparkled forth in the lives of communicants, so that others would say, "These have been with Jesus!" And their consciences may lie under the power of this conviction, that the sacrament has a confirming and a transforming virtue in it!

USE 4. Comfort to God's people.

1. From Christ's broken body and His blood poured out, we may gather this comfort, that it was a glorious sacrifice.

It was a sacrifice of infinite merit. Had it been only an angel that suffered, or had Christ been only a mere man, as some blasphemously dream, then we might have despaired of salvation. But He suffered for us who was God as well as man. Therefore, the apostle expressly calls it "the blood of God" (Acts 20:28). It is man that sins. It is God in our nature that dies. This is sovereign medicine to believers. Christ having poured out His blood, now God's justice is completely satisfied. God was infinitely more content with Christ's sufferings upon Mount Calvary than if we had lain in hell and undergone His wrath forever. The blood of Christ has quenched the flame of divine fury. And, now, what should we fear? All are enemies are either reconciled or subdued. God is a reconciled enemy, and sin is a subdued enemy. "Who shall lay anything to the charge of God's elect? It is Christ that died" (Romans 8:34). When the devil accuses us, let us show him the cross of Christ. When he brings his pencil and goes to paint our sin in their colors, let us bring the sponge of Christ's blood, and that will wipe them out again. All bonds are cancelled. Whatever the law has charged upon us is discharged. The debt book is crossed with the blood of the Lamb.

It was a sacrifice of eternal extent. The benefit of it is perpetuated. "He entered in once into the holy place, having obtained eternal redemption for us" (Hebrews 9:12). Therefore, Christ is said to be a Priest forever (Hebrews 5:6), because the virtue and comfort of His sacrifice abides forever.

2. Christ's blood being shed, believers may lay claim to all heavenly privileges. Wills are ratified by the death of the testator. "A testament is of force after men are dead" (Hebrews 9:17). It is observable in the text that Christ calls His blood "the blood of the New Testament." Christ made a will or testament, and gave rich legacies to the saints: pardon of sin, grace, and glory. The Scriptures are the rolls wherein these legacies are registered. Christ's blood is the sealing of the will. This blood being shed, Christians may put in for a title to these legacies.

"Lord, pardon my sin. Christ has died for my pardon. Give me grace; Christ has purchased it by His blood."

The testator being dead, the will is in force. Christian, are you not filled with joy? Are you not possessed of heaven? Yet you have this confirmed by will. A man who has a deed sealed, making over such lands and tenements after the expiration of a few years, though at present he has little to help himself with, yet he comforts himself when he looks upon his sealed deed with hopes of that which is to come. So though at present we do not enjoy the privileges of consolation and glorification, yet we may cheer our hearts with this: the deed is sealed; the will and testament is ratified by the blood shedding of Christ.

3. Is Christ's blood shed? Here is comfort against death. A dying Savior sweetens the pangs of death. Is your Lord crucified? Be of good comfort. Christ, by dying, has overcome death. He has cut the lock of sin where the strength of death lay. Christ has knocked out the teeth of this lion. He has pulled the thorn out of death so that it cannot prick a believer's conscience. "O death, I will be thy plague" (Hosea 13:14). Christ has disarmed death and taken away all its deadly weapons so that, though it may strike, it cannot sting a believer. Christ has drawn the poison out of death. Nay, He has made death friendly. This pale horse carries a child of God home to his Father's house. Faith gives a right to heaven; death gives us possession. What sweet comfort may we draw from the crucifixion of our Lord! His precious blood makes the pale face of death to be of a ruddy and beautiful complexion.

USE 5. Here is a dark side of the cloud to all profane persons who live and die in sin. They have no part in Christ's blood. Their condition will be worse than if Christ had not died. Christ, who is a lodestone to draw the elect to heaven, will be a millstone to sink the wicked deeper in hell. There is a crew of sinners who slight Christ's blood and swear by it. Let them know His blood will cry against them. They must feel the same wrath which Christ felt upon the cross. And, because they cannot bear it at once, they must be undergoing it to eternity (2 Thessalonians 1:9). So inconceivably torturing will this be that the damned do not know how to endure it, nor yet how to avoid it.

Sinners will not believe this until it is too late.

Wicked men, while they live, are blinded by the god of this world. But, when they are dying, the eye of their consciences will begin to be opened and they shall see the wrath of God flaming before their eyes, which sight will be but a sad prologue to an eternal tragedy.